THE COLUMBUS ANTHOLOGY

The Columbus Anthology

EDITED AND WITH AN INTRODUCTION
BY AMANDA PAGE

TRILLIUM, AN IMPRINT OF
THE OHIO STATE UNIVERSITY PRESS
COLUMBUS

BELT PUBLISHING
CLEVELAND

CONTENTS

Columbus

MAGGIE SMITH

When I pronounce my city's name,
the forgiveness I ask is silent.

Like all local schoolchildren,
I have seen the statue pointing

with its hard bronze hand.
And in the year of our lord 2017

I have called my representatives.
I have programmed their numbers

into my phone. I have called myself
a Columbus native without

considering what it means. What else
have I claimed that was not mine?

Buzzards teeter overhead
with wind-torn wings, those ragged

flags of no place in particular.
At the river, the replica Santa Maria

is docked and bobbing, ready
for a school bus to pull up. Light skips

x • THE COLUMBUS ANTHOLOGY

itself like a stone across the water.
I am calling again to tell the senator

we do not want to die. I am here
to speak. If my representative is out,

I will wait. Where have I called
home that was not home?

Introduction

AMANDA PAGE

Columbus, Ohio, is an interesting city. Those of us who live here have a lot to say about it. I've heard quips that Columbus "is a great place to live, but I wouldn't want to visit," and "to live in Columbus is to live with one foot out the door." I've heard residents shred the city for what it lacks, and I've heard residents gush with love for the lives they can lead here and only here. It is a city without an absolute and concrete place in the national imagination. It doesn't even really have one in the regional imagination. It is not technically a Rust Belt city, yet many people from the Rust Belt have come here and made a home. It is a capital city, built specifically for that duty and selected for its central location in the state of Ohio. It is a city that was intentionally designed, but has trouble designing a definitive identity, at least one packaged perfectly for national consumption. Many people who live here believe it does not matter that we convey a unified brand to the world. We are what we are. Others are defensive about our undefined image on the national stage. Sometimes, that defensiveness shows up in our local media. Every so often, I see a piece—an article, a podcast—that takes a defensive tone. I don't think it comes from a place of insecurity about the merits of the city. I think it comes from caring about what the city is and what it is becoming, for those of us living here, and those of us moving here (or moving back here) at an exceedingly rapid rate.

As the population grows, so does the number of conversations about Columbus. It is a city that talks about itself, amongst itself, and local media and artists shape the conversation daily. In their individual forms and formats, they ask, "What is Columbus?" They use specific pieces of culture in the city as a lens through which they might answer that question. Is the city defined by a sports team? A particular dish? A musical genre?

It is always up for discussion.

And the discussion gets broader and deeper with each new participant. New participants are coming to the city. Columbus could very much be viewed as a transient's city. We are a city of many people who left other places, often in search of something: a job, an education, a new start. As we come to the city, we see it with fresh eyes. We lend new voices to the old conversation.

I came here, for the first time, when I was nineteen. I drove up Route 23 from my southern Ohio hometown and pumped my fist in the air as I drove past the BP gas station, just before passing under 270 and entering the city at its southern point. That time, I stayed nine months. During those nine months, I had a shocking number of conversations about what the city was. The common refrain was, "Columbus will be great when it decides what it wants to be."

I came back after I graduated from college. That time, I stayed twenty months, and I had twice as many conversations about what Columbus was, and what it wanted to be.

I left again and was gone for twelve years. When I returned, new friends began to ask me what I thought of the city. New friends started to tell me what they thought Columbus might become.

I think that's the beauty of the city. The conversation continues. Maybe we're not having trouble designing a definitive identity. Maybe we are a city that is constantly considering what it will become. We are a city that lives in the discussion of what we could be.

We could be a city that defines ourselves through any one piece of our material culture. I think that would be too easy, though. In this anthology, there is no mention of the beer culture or ice cream in Columbus. College football isn't discussed. Our city's reputation as the penultimate American test market doesn't get explained at all. You won't get a full picture of the musical talent or incredible comic art that exists in Columbus (although you will get a taste). The sum of those parts does not a city make. Yet, each of those parts does make an indelible mark on the city's culture, its function and branding.

What you *will* get a sense of: the remarkable poetry scene. You will get a sense that many people move here, for many a reason. Many people who were born and raised here stay here, also for many a reason. You will get a sense of the significant nonfiction that comes from the writers in Columbus, many of whom are also poets. We work in many genres because we are not always willing to be defined by one thing, much like our city.

My hope is that this anthology is a volume one, and that in the years to come, we see subsequent collections of work from writers who call Columbus home, whether they moved here fifteen years ago or fifteen minutes ago. This is a collection of pieces that inform our perspective of who we are. We are presenting the possibilities to one another. We are asking the question, "What is Columbus?" We are asking the question, "What does Columbus want to be?" We are what we are talking about. We are what we could be.

Five Reasons Why Writers Should Move to Columbus

ANNIE McGREEVY

1. It's affordable.

Under a thousand dollars a month can get you a one-bedroom apartment smack in the center of the Short North, a popular gay neighborhood. There you're close to art galleries, ethnic restaurants, and hip breweries, like Seventh Son, that pay as much attention to the aesthetic of their space as they do to the taste of their beer, making it a lovely space to socialize at night by the firepit, or work quietly in the daytime. The North Market features Thai, Vietnamese, Mexican, Indian, Polish, Italian, and more, including the famous Jeni's Ice Cream. The very decent public transportation system means a car isn't an imperative, though once you've got one, parking and traffic aren't the headache they can be in cities of comparable size. We were ranked 34th in the nation for best places to bike, a great way to get around after a day of sitting and writing.

Ready to be a homeowner, you successful writer you? (Congratulations on your romance novel/vampire series/ very lucrative side gig with Mary Kay.) Established writers can buy a nice house in a safe neighborhood with a decent public school system. The median sale price in Columbus proper in 2014 was $141,500, and in 2015 it was $126, 900, so go ahead and cash in that advance and go nuts at Ikea.

What this affordability looks like: if you come here for grad school, your crippling self-doubt and alcohol problems can play out in the privacy of a decent one bedroom or a run-down half a duplex on your stipend, within walking distance of grocery stores, bars, restaurants, and parks.

2. There's a plethora of part-time opportunities perfect for creative people.

Being an adjunct English instructor isn't ideal if you have an expectation of the American Dream. But if your goal is to make enough money to live, have enough time to write, and feel intellectually engaged, there are a half-dozen colleges and universities that keep the Columbus literati regularly employed. Most of these positions are to teach composition, which I like to think less as a distraction from creative writing and more of intellectual and artistic cross-training—important to a writing routine and a relief.

The stories we tell ourselves, right?!

At Columbus College of Art & Design, adjunct instructors regularly teach creative writing workshops, for a decent wage, too. At Columbus State Community College, you don't need a lengthy CV to teach creative classes, but you do have to teach about a hundred students to make a living wage.

An adjunct English instructor at The Ohio State University makes approximately $5,000 a class. If you don't have a car payment or student loans, and you really like ramen, you can live off of a class or two (I did this in 2011 and 2012) and write most of the livelong day.

At Columbus State Community College, the salary is significantly less than OSU, and CCAD is somewhere in between. In the suburbs, you can teach at Dennison or Otterbein and make more, though these opportunities are harder to come by.

3. There is just enough to do, but not too much.

I didn't always love Columbus. In 2011, a group of writer friends and I were joking about the city's campaign to come up with a new slogan. "Come Settle Here," one suggested. "Columbus: Everything You Need and Nothing More," another said. Now I think about that second one fondly.

Everything about Columbus is Midwestern: the city is polite, wants to stay out of your way, endeavors not to distract you. The weather keeps you working inside all winter, curled up with a candle and a book while the snow falls, and then gives you just enough hiking/camping/cookout opportunities in the other seasons. But it by no means demands that you get out there and enjoy it. The city gives you ways to distract yourself from your impending death on an introvert's rhythm:

There are excellent dance parties just about every weekend: hip-hop, pop, and vinyl oldies. In their Midwestern way, they don't compete with one another. There's even a Friday early-morning dance party called "Wake and Shake" at Wild Goose Creative where you can unselfconsciously get down and sweat out some of that existential dread before you even start your day. The Wexner Center brings in fascinating art installations every six months and hosts an outdoor film series in the summer.

The local music scene is absolutely killer: for five dollars or less on a weeknight, you can see a great show, and the city attracts headliners of all genres too. Venues like Ace of Cups, Strongwater, Newport Music Hall, Notes, and Bluestone host local bands like Counterfeit Madison and Saintseneca, selling out of tickets quickly.

In the last decade the following authors have spoken for free in central locations: Dave Eggers, Sue Miller, Richard Bausch, Zadie Smith, Junot Diaz, Michael Chabon, Eula Biss, Sharon Olds, Jamaal May, Terrence Hays, Brenda Hillman, Salman Rushdie, Michael Ondaatje, Bell Hooks, Sherman Alexie, Natasha Tretheway, Ann Patchett, Percival Everett, Angela Davis, Edward P. Jones, Ta-Nahesi Coates, Roxane Gay, Bell Hooks, Claire Vaye Watkins, Natalie Diaz, Stuart Dybeck, Scott Raab, Tobias Wolff, Billy Collins, Jennifer Egan, Jonathan Franzen, Sarah Shun-Lien Bynum, Harryette Mullen, Anne Carson, Meghan Daum, Claudia Emerson.

The city boasts a handful of reading series for the up and coming too, often paired with established local writers (of which there are plenty) as well as a thriving Slam Poetry scene.

4. There's a big LGBTQIA community here, and activism is strong.

Here in Columbus, people give a shit. Several nights a week, there are talks or meetups to try to make the city better, more accessible, more connected, safer for everyone. Activists and local politicians are friendly in coffee shops, and the city is small enough that you run into people. The queer community is integral, with some describing us as the next San Francisco.

Black Lives Matter Columbus has an active chapter here as well, and they do the work of educating the community on the work still left to be done. Which, as we know, is considerable.

Writers need to strike a balance between solitude and connectedness, and being literally alone and truly understanding other people, and Columbus is the perfect place for that.

5. It's not New York or L.A.

Or Paris. Or Prague. It's distinctly uncool, in the literary sense, and this is precisely what makes it so cool. What are you a writer for, if not to discover something unknown? If not to see something that is under-documented and bring it out into the world? I'm not saying such creation is impossible in your Nigerias and your Irelands, but sometimes a little less competition can be a good thing. Yes, there is an army of fundamental-Christian-looking-hipsters in flannel shirts and bushy beards, and they will talk your ear off about craft beer and their new fixed-gear bike that they built with their grandpa's tools. But true pretension is hard to come by here, and that's seriously valuable to a writer, budding or established. There are plenty of people to talk shop with, but no one judges you when you're agentless, publicationless, broke, or in a dry spell. There is a serious camaraderie here, and a lovely lack of pressure.

Here we're not on the cutting edge of anything, except medicine, college football, and deciding who the next leader of the free world will be.

Come Settle Here.

Buckeye to All That

MANDY SHUNNARAH

When my six-hour delayed flight arrived at CMH, it was nearly 2:30 a.m. The small airport where I had my layover had closed all of its restaurants at 8:00 p.m.—airports being the miserable places they are—so when the wheels hit the tarmac at Port Columbus, all I could think about was food.

My sleep-deprived partner picked me up and declared the Waffle House outside the airport "too dangerous." I didn't ask what that meant. He grew up in Columbus, so I took his word for it. Instead, he suggested Buckeye Donuts.

"I don't want donuts. You know I don't even like sugary stuff. I need real food."

"They've got the best Greek food in town at this hour. Get a gyro or something," he said.

Against all logic, a place called Buckeye Donuts served Greek food. Falafel right alongside bear claws; shawarma dotting the menu next to apple fritters. To add more mystery to the madness, the place was set up like a '50s diner, with a lunch counter and red leather barstools.

It was clear Buckeye Donuts had gone through many iterations, standing the test of time and taking a little of the past into each new chapter of the future. Buckeye Donuts was paying homage to its roots by being unabashedly eclectic.

If a place like that could thrive in Columbus, maybe I could too.

I'm a half Palestinian child in a family of Alabama rednecks. I'm the bookworm in a family of non-readers. I'm the college grad in a family of mostly high school dropouts. I'm an electric blue dot in a fiery red family. I'm an atheist in a family of believers. I know what it is to feel chronically out of place, a square peg in a round hole.

My hometown, Birmingham, Alabama, never felt like home. From the time I was 12, I longed for the day I'd turn 18 so I could run away to New York City and make my way as a writer. To prepare, I'd watch cartoons like *Hey, Arnold* with pen in hand, making notes on navigating the bus system, the time the streetlights came on and signaled the kids' curfew, and the Stoop Kid who never leaves his stoop.

To the children on the show, Stoop Kid was an anomaly—a neighborhood fixture as curious and strange as the street performer and corner tarot reader. But Stoop Kid made sense to me. If I lived in a place like New York City, where endless throngs of beautiful and fascinating people passed by and I could have anything my imagination conjured delivered to my door, I'd never leave my stoop either.

It was a plan forged in naiveté. When Joan Didion wrote "was anyone ever so young?" she was talking about me. By the time I was 18, I was forced into the responsibility that comes with age. Without a full ride and generous support from my family (who would've preferred me to marry my high school sweetheart, have a snot-nosed kid or two, and tease old women's perms for a living), those NYC universities would be impossible without crippling debt.

So I stayed in Birmingham, a daily reminder of my fear, guilting myself for letting a chance to escape pass me by. When my best friend dropped out of college to follow the siren's song of the city, I swore I'd follow upon graduation. But New

York requires money—money I didn't have. Not after the small media startup I worked at closed the same week I graduated. I found myself jobless and homeless in the same week and spent the little funds I had loafing around on friend's couches—in Birmingham, Chicago, Oxford, Mississippi, Athens, Georgia, and Murray, Kentucky, where I relied on the kindness of my then-boyfriend's wealthy parents.

Making money writing was harder than I could have imagined, especially when the only clips to my name were in small-town newspapers, sarcastic alt-weeklies, and a defunct online magazine with an expiration date on its domain registration.

Before I met my partner, I hadn't given Columbus much thought. Without the legendary associations like "writers: NYC" and "actors: LA," I couldn't place it. Columbus didn't occupy the space in my mind where I filed things I needed to achieve my dream of being a writer, so I assumed the city had nothing for me. I thought Columbus was just another part of flyover country, a useless expanse of land between the places that mattered; places where you could go to really be someone.

But after visiting for a week, with my partner as tour guide, the city endeared itself to me.

Columbus is distinctly Midwestern, straddling the line between the South, where I grew up, and the new identity I wanted to create.

As someone who had never previously lived outside Alabama, the Midwest was a comforting blend of familiar and foreign. The Ohio State agricultural program's cattle farm in the middle of the city felt familiar since you don't have to go too far outside Birmingham before you hit wide open expanses of land. The willingness of people to talk to strangers in public places was even more pronounced than the "Southern hospitality" to which I was accustomed. I'd see grocery store coupons torn from the Sunday *Columbus Dispatch* placed on top of that item in the store, there for anyone to use. A neighbor put out a TV on the sidewalk and went through the effort to make a sign letting passersby know it did indeed work, they'd just gotten a newer model. An elderly woman at the grocery store, seeing me struggle to bag the bosomful of avocados I'd loaded up, took them one by one from my arms and tied them up in a plastic produce bag. A woman who walked to a yard sale at the home of my in-laws-to-be was offered a ride home when her purchases were too many to carry.

The foreignness often came to me on a plate. Delicacies like rhubarb pie, pierogies, and candy buckeyes are scarce in the South. It came, also, in sports—the Columbus Blue Jackets, specifically—since Alabama rarely sees ice or hockey, much less both of them together.

The foreignness came, too, in my ability to be alone. Having only ever lived in my hometown until I moved to Columbus, there was always a steady stream of friends to be seen and actions I must perform to maintain relationships. I was in the unhealthy habit of wanting to be the best possible best friend to all my friends, which left me feeling drained, burned out, and lacking time to write. In Columbus, I could choose to limit the number of friends I acquired and manage my social interactions more carefully.

The magic some people associate with New York City is what I now feel when I think about Columbus. New York is a love affair, fleeting and temporary—one that can't compete with the stable, responsible city of home on a long-term basis. Columbus is the city that allowed me to escape and welcomed me, as I am, with open arms. In Columbus, I can afford to be an up-and-coming writer, one currently making zero dollars and zero cents from her work. I can afford to write here because I'm not bankrupted by skyrocketing rent and I'm not wearing myself down just trying to get by with the bare minimum.

My best friend had gone to New York to be a Broadway star, and after countless auditions where he was one of thousands for even the smallest parts, after the soaring rent even in the most squalid apartments, after the broken-down trains that left him late for work (for which he was eventually fired), and the general struggle of simply trying to survive, he and his partner announced they were leaving. It took four years, but they'd had enough.

Because hotel prices there are astronomical and I always stayed with them when I visited, I knew I wouldn't be going on annual trips to NYC anymore. At first I grieved the dream I knew now would never come true for me. I couldn't see myself living in Manhattan as a full-time writer anymore. My best friend is made of stronger stuff—if the city wore him down to a nub, it would do worse to me.

Like so many who fall victim to its charms, I was never able to see New York City for what it was—a rat-infested, roach-covered concrete jungle with litter-strewn streets where no one but the 1% could afford to live comfortably. When I visited, I never stayed long enough to have to lug an armload of groceries up five flights of stairs or attempt to arrive at work on time using the crumbling subway. NYC, at present, is a place for tourists—a place to visit and leave before you get too tired or too old to find joy in its thrills.

Birmingham was a different story. I was always able to see Birmingham for what it was—a city that often sent its best and brightest packing by squashing any hope of progress with the unstoppable tide of corruption and rampant racism.

I look at Columbus with older, more scrutinous eyes, and I see a city of active participants. I see labor organizers encouraging people to boycott the hometown fast-food chain Wendy's for exploiting farmworkers. I see people sheltering immigrant families from ICE. I see people hanging red ribbon-festooned coat hangers on the fence outside the statehouse when the Republican-majority legislature threatens to limit reproductive rights. I see people who refuse to sit idly when injustice strikes because they know Columbus isn't perfect, but they love their city enough to demand better of it. I see people not conforming to the idea of what Columbus wants them to be. Instead, they are creating the city they want—one that accommodates all that they are.

Despite what I'd once thought, "Midwestern" doesn't mean devoid of culture, but rather the Midwest has its own distinct culture; one so often glossed over in favor of the allure of big city bright lights. Columbus is no New York City, but it's no Birmingham either. And it's in that in-between space—between my comfort zone and the bright, shiny promise of newness—where I found myself at home.

And if I want to see hoards of beautiful young people and feel the rush of the crowd on the sidewalk, there's always the university district—as long as Ohio State's classes are in session.

After I processed the announcement that my best friend and his partner would be LA-bound upon leaving New York, I said what only someone who loves her home could:

"Y'all should come to Columbus."

"We just might do that one of these days," he replied.

"When you get here, the first place I'm taking you is Buckeye Donuts . . . I know it's going to sound crazy, but they've got the best gyros in town. Trust me on this one."

I'm Here to Win

HARMONY COX

I was born in Columbus, and it's becoming increasingly likely that I will die here. Not because of any kind of conspiracy (though, really, you can't rule out that kind of thing), but because I am at a point in my life where I'm unlikely to resettle. I'm too angry and shy to make new friends, I think public transportation is overrated, and I've finally perfected my green bean casserole recipe. Columbus it is!

I kid, a little bit. But every native Columbusite does. When we hang out, our collective inferiority complex tends to flare up. There's an edge to our jokes about our old stomping grounds, a real disdain for the kind of people this town has made us. Can you believe we used to actually eat the bagels at Bernie's? (Did you see Wesley Willis there? Which time? It was INSANE.) Can you believe we used to tolerate the smell of Nag Champa just to buy shitty records at Magnolia Thunderpussy? Our eyes grow wide and frantic, and everything we say is punctuated by an unspoken question: why are we still here? Why were we abandoned by the post-college rapture that transported our friends and family to better, cooler cities? Why were we the last ones to hear about kale?!

I won't mince words: this town hasn't always felt like home. It's a small blue city in a big red state, and even the most liberal folks have values that tend towards the traditional. I've always felt too fat, too poor, and too awkward to blend in with my fellow citizens. I never learned how to pretend to like the things that other people like. I don't understand how football works and I'm never going to try. I'm a liberal feminist and I don't pull my punches. I play Dungeons and Dragons on the regular. I'm not in the mix when it comes to idealized small-town people. It's lucky for me that as you grow up you realize that nobody actually "fits in," and the people with mainstream tastes and the ability to make small talk often feel just as alienated as you do. Once you realize that it's the same for everyone, it's liberating. It frees you to let some things go and make your life into what you want it to be.

I don't envy people who live in New York anymore. I envy women my size who have the confidence to wear tank tops. It's not because I've lowered my standards; it's because I've realized there's nothing in another city that makes me better than I am now. I'm good with what I already have, and what I have are huge arms and a low tolerance for heat, so it's time to break out the sunscreen and reassess my life goals as a newly dedicated citizen of my hometown.

There's nothing wrong with leaving if that's where your heart is. If you set your feet down in another city and it feels like home, you should stay there instead. But there's something special about the tough weirdos who stay in the Midwest. We have to work harder to find the good books, the good music, the good stuff that people in bigger cities take for granted. Bands usually end up here by accident, and every damn show is on a Tuesday night because it's the only time they can squeeze us in between Detroit and Pittsburgh. We're the easy punchline for every coastal city jagoff with a grudge against the hicks in the "flyover" states. Politicians and demagogues hold us up as the standard bearers for backwards values and discriminatory laws that only a handful of our neighbors actually support. Football happens every stupid year and it never fucking ends. Until we find each other, it's easy to feel alone.

But there are rewards! Once you get over yourself, you see cool people making things on every corner, and a seat at the table for you if you want it. The things you love you truly love, and the things you create are truly your own. I have spent much of my life not trying to create or be anything because I thought it wasn't for me. I thought I had to live somewhere else, be someone else, to be special. I've recently realized how stupid and selfish that is. I want to tell stories, even if they're small and selfish, just because they're mine. What's stopping me, aside from crippling social anxiety and self doubt?

DC can brag about inventing punk rock, but the Midwest invented the kind of people who need it: people who got made fun of all day at school and then ran home and slammed their bedroom doors and spent the hours till dinner staring out the window and memorizing the words to every song on *Combat Rock*. People that have a lot of anger and a lot of hope in their big bleeding rustbelt hearts. People who channel the insane Midwestern work ethic into hustling their own angry art. People who are determined to be the best part of a city that doesn't quite know what to do with them but gives them a home anyway. Punks and weirdos and loners become the outstretched hands of hope scattered throughout our small towns. There are plenty of backwards assholes, sure, but we're all here too. We're all still here.

Art in a City That Can Kill You

SCOTT WOODS

To my fellow Columbus black creatives,

For a while now, but especially in the wake of yet another police acquittal, we have needed to come to a decision about this city.

We have a particular relationship with Columbus when it comes to how we are treated by the state. It is a relationship that goes back numerous generations, and in every era of Columbus's development has ended with black communities receiving the short end of the stick. I can list all of the neighborhoods I'm referring to, but they're the same neighborhoods we talk about every time we talk about gentrification and police abuse and political capital and the school system. You know them and I know them, and the people who live in those areas now know them, even as they put up new signs and light arches. We have a relationship with Columbus, and once you do the math, I don't think it's hyperbole to suggest it's abusive by every measure.

While Columbus houses nearly 900,000 residents, the city is not so large that your chances of escaping the effects of a given murder or abuse of another black resident are high. When these crimes happen, you likely know someone who knows whom it happened to. Most of us are probably only three or four people removed from a victim of police abuse or murder in this city, regardless of where you live or how many white friends you have. And the more invested you are in the culture and politics of black people in Columbus, the more likely that awareness is.

Think about why that's true. Are black people preternaturally social? Do we have designated meeting spots where we gather en masse and trade culture and intel? No, and of course not, respectively. We often connect to our victims through our people because when you live under conditions designed for your destruction, you regularly engage others that you assume can relate to your condition. Survivors typically seek out other survivors for mental and emotional support, especially under what could easily be labeled fog of war conditions. Under such a state, you remain constantly aware of the targets you might know, the people who notice you for what you are when you walk into a room without knowing who you are, as you have done in kind.

We are a valuable people. Sure, all lives matter, but we bring things that other people and institutions find valuable beyond our lives. You can hear the import they place on those things every day, see it in how others treat what we create, represent, and provide above and beyond the offerings of others. They love our music, our art, our fashion, our language, our bodies, our abilities. At the same time they fear our presence, our knowing looks, our potential, our language, our bodies, our abilities.

What we provide is valuable in a literal sense as well. It is no coincidence that when it comes time to sell Columbus to the world, we are frequently held up to seal the deal. "Look how diverse we are!" the billboards suggest. "Look how much culture we possess!" What we generate—frequently without the aid of tax dollars—is oftentimes the very key to a city's ability to unlock more tax dollars, which every developing city needs.

For all of these reasons black artists need to decide if Columbus is worthy of our efforts. We need to decide if we will remain satisfied to make statements in our art or if other types of statements need to be delivered, other actions taken. We need to make those decisions individually and, when possible and sound, collectively. We need to decide if our goal is to point fingers or to lift hands. We need to decide if we're willing to keep giving the best of ourselves to the worst of our opposition, if we're going to continue to resign ourselves to being gentrified out of the city, ignored by 90% of the politicians we install, dismayed at the way our schools treat our children, terrorized by a police state, and living off of the scraps of the in-the-know, the hip, and the well-meaning. Does a city deserve to not only take credit but benefit in key ways from the efforts of the artists it maligns when they aren't being artists (and sometimes when they are)? How much of the culture we generate does Columbus get to take credit for, beyond being a well of inspiration of the worst kind? Do people assume we enjoy painting our conditions, creating poetry about our collective demise, and choreographing our oppression? Is the nature poem ever beyond the ken of our poets? Must our rappers never find love in their bars?

We have conversations to have, and then we have decisions to make. We all have to live somewhere. Lord knows a lot of the places where one can attempt to build a life and career with their art aren't much better, and are frequently worse. This isn't a call to leave Columbus. This is a call to reconsider our relationship. We are not a powerless people at large, and our artists are even more steeled to show the way than ever before. Art is always at the front line of change. The question I place before you now is: who gets to benefit from the changes we are making?

Every Day I Ride the Bus

DAVID BREITHAUPT

It starts with a smell.

It is 8:22 a.m. on a weekday. I am heading downtown on the No. 8 COTA bus, not quite awake as usual, nor still asleep. I take my seat, and an odor awakens me. I scan my fellow passengers for suspects, but first, I make sure it's not me and discreetly raise my arm to check. I pass the test.

Sitting at the front of the bus are two suspects. Mind you, I'm an open-minded passenger and I give everyone a fair shake, but sitting at the front of the bus are two riders consuming my attention. The first is very suspicious, a large white woman in a wheelchair that has been strapped to the side of the bus. Her skin has a pale white coloring with tints of pink and blue, the kind of shade you see on a body pulled from the river after two days. Her hair is a crazy kind of chemical perm, the indestructible kind, in bluish gray hues. Slung around one of the handles of her chair is a plastic bag filled with Depends. This is ominous evidence, but as I said, I am keeping an open mind.

But first, the *smell.* Here it is: an odor of cat urine, that unmistakable smell, which for me, evokes childhood memories of a neighbor's house that overflowed with cats. The fumes hold me in limbo between past and present. I yearn for nostalgia and curse the present. Or do I have it backwards? I think I curse them both. The push and pull between the two makes me slightly dizzy. I can only hope the smell doesn't stick to my clothes.

The second suspect is a large man who is twitching and jerking. His hair is long and black and he stares forward with that look white people ascribe to native wisdom. He might have MS, Parkinson's or Tourette's syndrome. Or maybe he has ridden the bus for too many years. He is impeccable, a man of dignity. I can't see him losing control of his bodily functions. He percolates, while seemingly meditating, watching his own thought forms rise. I don't know, I'm just going with my instincts. I vote for the wheelchair woman. She looks like the Purina Cat Chow Lady, and that just about settles it for me. And then there is the Depends . . .

The odor envelopes me like a fog rolling into the bay. I'm dazed. The man behind me is drinking alcohol. I can smell it, but it is not nearly enough to combat the urine smell. I hear the drinker say to his seatmate, "It has orange juice in it, it's a breakfast drink!"

As I catalog the morning scents, I can hear the riders moaning and swaying like seasick passengers on a cruise boat. I think of mustard gas and WWI. I think of the holocaust. I am not trivializing those two beyond-tragic events, but as I ride the bus this morning, those thoughts race through my mind. I picture bodies collapsing, giant common graves, glue factories, baby diapers. I retreat three seats back.

"Plenty of vitamin C," says the breakfast drinker, nodding his head in self confirmation.

We are still on High Street, stopped at Stewart alongside a McDonald's. The driver opens the door and flees outside. "Back in five," she shouts as she runs toward McDonald's, not stopping until she is inside.

"Bathroom break," someone mutters. "Formal retreat," says another. Several riders take advantage to exit, wait on the curb, and light up a cigarette. Exclamations of relief fill the air.

I look to see what effect this is having on the Purina Cat Chow Lady. She stares ahead, oblivious of any commotion. The Native American twitches and sits, unmoved. I take advantage of the retreat and move back a few more seats.

The driver is certainly taking her time. What if she passed out and died in the restroom? What is the appropriate amount of time to wait before sending in a rescue team?

Some of the smokers are on their second cigarette. Time measured in smokes, nicotine clocks.

Plumes of smoke are drifting back into the bus, causing a medley of olfactory sensations. It is a public transit bouquet with hints of tobacco, Mad Dog, and *eau du chat*. The combination is exotic.

The bus driver finally reappears, and the smokers stub out their cigs and reboard. After twenty minutes, we have made it only a few blocks up High Street. The stress of overwhelming odors and the ongoing bathroom break seems to make time stand still. I panic, wondering if I would ever get to work, that perhaps I had died and this was my hell, riding a stinky COTA bus for eternity. It seems the right punishment for me.

Where does the sense of smell rank in the order of survival tools? It is certainly primary in the animal kingdom. In the world of humans, it may rank third after sight and hearing. I don't know for sure. This is not my field of expertise. It serves mostly as a footnote to denote whether something is bad or good. Flowers are good; they smell nice. Dog poop is bad; it smells awful. I remember a line some Frenchman wrote in a book called *The Physiology of Taste* (read it for a French cuisine class) in which he declared, "Without the participation of smell, there is no taste." This is a bad moment to recall that line, as I do not wish to think about assigning a taste to this smell. Makes me stifle a gag reflex. Best to move on.

One by one the riders exit at their stops as if propelled by an invisible force. They are like corks popping off a champagne bottle. I can see their relief as they soak in the oxygen of the street. I look on in envy; I have a few stops to go.

Outside my window I can see the shopping cart guy, thin with a gnarled gray beard, pushing his worldly possessions in a commandeered cart. He is always at the same spot every day and waves at us with a happy and energetic smile. Shopping cart guy has a secret knowledge.

The usual Columbus facades roll by, the Daily Growler, the Republic Café, White Castle. In the distance I can see the LeVeque Tower—I am almost where I need to be.

Swole for the Revolution

MERYL WILLIAMS

I've been bad at roller derby in three different states, but Ohio Roller Derby taught me how to hit back the hardest. When I moved back home to Ohio just in time to vote in a swing state in the fall of 2016, I had no idea how much I was going to need the strength they were about to give me.

Living in a red state requires a decent temperament and sense of humor, but it also suggests that you know how to stick up for yourself. Resistance looks different in Columbus, a blue dot in a sea of red, and being confronted with views you don't share gets you out of your comfort zone more often. Luckily, roller derby got me in the practice of being uncomfortable before all of politics set itself on fire two years ago.

I started skating in 2015 when I was living in Chicago. I joined up with a group of women in Oak Park, Illinois, in the western suburbs, right after a breakup but also right after starting a new job that allowed me to finally buy roller derby gear. The group was a mix of retired derby players and newbies, and I was planted well in the latter category. The retirees were kind and welcoming of me and the others who didn't yet know how to skate backwards or what a pace line was.

Six months later, I moved to Portland, Oregon, mercifully keeping the job, but still escaping the breakup. Even though I had a good network in Chicago and skating was a salve, I wanted to get out of the city I'd shared with my former partner. Moving to the West Coast felt like a big reset button.

I made it 15 months. After a humbling tryout with the Rose City Rollers rec league, I realized I was way out of my element. My Chicago crowd had been warm and welcoming, but Portland was almost too big to make a place within. Still, part of me knows I got discouraged early on and didn't try hard enough after that. Portland's roller derby league is one of the biggest in the world, and while they had a startup program for new folks, it had to compete with the big league players for practice time. I was told to come to practice once a week, at 8 a.m. on Sundays. As someone in their 20s who was going out every Saturday night with new friends, it wasn't ideal.

Portland was not ideal either, it turned out. When I moved there, it was July, and the summer stretched on well into October. But when the rainy season started, I realized I'd overestimated my tolerance for the gray skies and drizzly weather of the Pacific Northwest. I'd told everyone I'd be fine with it, but it turned out to be pretty oppressive after six months straight. By April, even though the clouds were finally parting, I hadn't carved out a space for myself like I'd pictured, and I knew it was time to go back home.

Before Chicago, I'd moved to Columbus after graduating from Muskingum University, located an hour or so east. Even as I was leaving Ohio, I told everyone I knew I'd be back someday, since I'm a native—I just wasn't sure when. In Portland, after being three time zones away on the West Coast, I felt ready. I moved back to Columbus in the fall, and tryouts for Ohio Roller Derby were the following week—six days before the 2016 presidential election. Finding out that I made the team felt like the last good news I'd get for a while.

I had missed feeling like part of a team. I'd gotten away from my ex by leaving Chicago, but that had also meant saying goodbye to weekly nachos and beer after practice in Lombard at the brew pub near the roller rink. In Portland, while I'd easily made friends outside of roller derby, I didn't make friends with teammates the way I'd let myself believe I instantly would. I stopped going to practice there altogether, but I missed it.

By the time I got back to Columbus, I still hadn't played in a proper scrimmage and didn't have much experience hitting or blocking. But now in my "new" Central Ohio city, I didn't even yet know what all I didn't know. Ohio Roller Derby had to build me from the ground up, but the veterans there welcomed the challenge. It was more or less my first rodeo, but it was hardly theirs.

Formerly called the Ohio Roller Girls (OHRG), the Columbus-based league was one of a handful of original leagues in the Women's Flat Track Derby Association (WFTDA), a now international coalition of roller derby leagues. My rookie season was their 12th. You'd think they'd have been tired of training newbies at that point, but the veteran skaters seemed excited to share their knowledge with people willing to learn. My rookie class had nine skaters, and I remember more than once when vets like Lorraine Acid or Chainsaw would stay after, showing the rookies footwork exercises off skates, or sharing good workouts for bad knees.

"You go like this," said Acid one night after practice, when it was already dark outside, as she jumped gingerly on the fronts of her sneakers. She gracefully circled the base of a tree outside our southside practice space while my teammate Birch Slap and I tried to mirror her movements, giggling nervously.

Foxy Force, the longest-running player in the whole league, once took time on a Sunday with me and another rookie at an outdoor skate park to help us practice speed and endurance so we could pass our skating laps test.

But nothing stuck with me more than the words of Lora "OutaMy" Wayman. Our tryouts process had included an interview portion "to make sure you're not an asshole," as we'd been told, and we'd all talked about our previous roller derby experience. I admitted I still didn't know how to hit or block, and mumbled something about how I really wasn't very athletic.

"I'm definitely not an athlete," I'd concluded, worrying that this painful admission would rule me out of the running.

Days later, after Wayman had left a voicemail on my phone telling me I'd made the team, I saw her at a bar for a roller derby bout watch party. The 2016 WFTDA championship game was on, and Portland's Rose City Rollers were playing New York's Gotham Girls for the Hydra Trophy. I stayed quiet while we watched what was technically my former league dominate. At halftime, Wayman sat down beside me.

"It's cool of you to come to this," she said, noting that I was one of a few rookies who came, even though we didn't know anyone yet. "I know it's tough when you're new."

I've never had much trouble meeting new people in new cities, but I appreciated what she was saying. Then, she spoke again.

"I've been thinking about what you said at tryouts, about not being an athlete," she said. "That's bullshit. You play roller derby, you are an athlete."

I've thought about Wayman saying that at least once a week since, usually in the pits of misery of a bad practice when I feel like I can't do anything right.

I'm not a skilled player, but Ohio Roller Derby worked with me anyway, making me better and faster all the same. The timing of the 2016 election mapping perfectly onto my rookie season played a factor as well, because the news of a swift political change for the country left many of us in need of an outlet that not just tolerated, but embraced, angry women. Calling legislators and marching in protests was important, but so was making my body tougher, it seemed. I raised protest signs downtown and on OSU's campus high above my shoulders, which I could feel were growing stronger every week.

We used to tell each other in car rides to practice, driving south from Clintonville, that we needed to "get swole for the revolution," as if we needed to be in peak physical shape in order to truly resist. I think it was half a joke, but the other half was a mantra.

In roller derby, you're constantly being told to get low to the ground, and to stay low. This form keeps your center of gravity in check, making you, as a player, harder to knock down. I became known for how low to the ground I could get when I skated. I would make an entire lap around the track, my butt inches from the ground, and then pull myself back up to full height. I did squats to keep in that shape, roughly counting myself down at the gym or even in my own living room. At practice, I would find I could spend two hours sweating and pushing, making my body move with force, and then realize after that I hadn't thought about politics at all, not even once. The same could not be said for any other two-hour periods of non-practice days, when I scrolled numbly through Twitter and refreshed the *Washington Post*'s website anxiously.

At practice, I felt myself getting more sturdy and confident on wheels, but I still struggled to hit other players hard enough to make an impact. That changed when I learned my signature move.

One weekend that season, we had a clinic with a visiting skater named Sarah Hipel, from another league. It was an all-day training in mid-April; it was humid, and North Korea was broadcasting to the U.S. that it was ready for war if necessary. Airstrikes were happening in Syria, Sean Spicer had just tried to convince the American people that Hitler never used chemical weapons, and Steve Bannon was still somehow important and dangerous. We were tired and hot, but we were there for practice anyway.

Sarah showed us some moves for "juking," when you fake out your opponent by making them incorrectly guess which direction you'll be going next. Then she added onto the move, by showing how you could trick your enemy by changing direction, but also hurt them in the process, by getting low to ground and then popping back up to hit them as you change route at the last second. As soon as I saw Sarah crouch down the way I'd been doing, I knew I wanted to master this trick. It was a simple move, but one I'd never seen before. I tried it that day and hit my practice partner squarely with my shoulder as I streaked past, knocking them out of my way. Pushing up with my shoulders instead of over, using my hips, turned out to be key for me, and I thought about the signs I raised above them in protest during the weeks and months before.

I may have become a one-trick pony, but I could finally give a hit as well as I could take one.

Living and skating in three different cities and states is an experience I wouldn't give back. It's still fun to visit Chicago and Portland and see my old teammates play, and I'm glad for the perspective I was granted by each. But nothing can change the fact that Ohio has always felt the most like home. It's here where my family can come see me play without hopping a plane, and I can teach my nieces how to skate at the same roller rink where I learned. It's here where I know three dozen teammates I can call if I want to support the Parkland students' efforts downtown in a local March for Our Lives. And it's here where I know I can learn in an environment in which everyone knows we're all just learning, and trying to do better.

Columbus is a place full of badass women, and they showed me that I am as well. And it's a place that has always known how to land a hit.

Thanks to the city, I finally do, too.

The Blue Jackets Have Turned Columbus into a Major League City

JEFF SVOBODA

What is Columbus, Ohio?

It's the kind of question cities have to ask themselves all the time. The only thing constant in life is that everything changes, and good cities constantly have to be asking themselves honest questions about what they are, what they want to be and how to get there.

To me, for the last decade or so, Columbus has been the hottest city in Ohio. Cleveland (downtown, the Flats) and Cincinnati (historic Over-the-Rhine and a built-up river district) have made major recent strides, but for consistency's sake, the state capital has been the heart of "The Heart of It All."

The numbers back it up. The city's metro area passed 2 million residents in 2015, putting Columbus on nearly even footing with Cleveland and Cincinnati, Ohio's traditional lead cities. Last year, some studies even suggested the area could have 3 million residents by 2050.

This is not a recent trend. Census figures show that from 1990 to 2010, the Columbus metro area saw its population increase by more than 30 percent. Cincinnati's metro area, meanwhile, grew around 15 percent, while Cleveland's actually dropped.

With an estimate of more than 850,000 residents within the city's borders in 2015, Columbus sits 15th in the nation and first in Ohio for population, and it's the second biggest media market in the state and 32nd overall.

In other words, Columbus is a legit big city, one becoming bigger and more legit each day.

I say all this to bring up two major points.

First, much of this is possible because of the Columbus Blue Jackets.

Certainly, not all of it. There are plenty of factors in play. With a more modern economy than either of the port cities in northeast and southwest Ohio, Columbus has grown organically over the past 25 years.

But I don't think you can overstate what the Jackets have done for the city and its image. A major league city has to have major league sports, and the Jackets were the city's entry ticket into the top four sports leagues in North America.

I didn't grow up in Columbus, but as someone who spent more than a decade living there, I read the recent book "Chill Factor" with interest. It all seems so obvious now that Columbus is a major league city, but two decades ago, there were many—everyday residents and power brokers alike—who didn't have the vision to see what was to come.

The fight to build a downtown arena and bring a pro team to the area was arduous and nearly sank multiple times, dragged down by those who saw Columbus only as a cowtown or a Buckeye town. The eventual victory came largely thanks to a handful of visionaries, chief among them John H. McConnell and Nationwide Insurance.

The renaissance of Columbus's self-image was also physical. Where a broken-down penitentiary once sat, one of the nation's premier athletic facilities grew. It's not a stretch to link the downtown Arena District to almost every major development in the city's heart over the past two decades, from the construction of Huntington Park to the explosion of living options to the steady progress of the Short North that reaches all the way to the Ohio State campus.

Simply put, the Arena District—and by proxy, the Blue Jackets—has been central to one of the great urban redevelopment success stories in the 21st century.

Which doubles back to my second point. Not only did the Blue Jackets help make Columbus a major league city, but the Blue Jackets will likely remain the city's only major league team.

With teams in both Cleveland and Cincinnati, neither Major League Baseball nor the National Football League are going to be awarding Columbus an expansion team anytime soon. The NBA isn't falling over itself to come to the capital, either. (Yes, we love the Crew, but we're sticking with the four traditional major sports here.)

This leaves Columbus as an underserved pro sports market. It's no secret why the Cleveland Browns have repeatedly looked at the city to host its training camp. It's also no secret why the Cleveland Indians linked up with the Columbus Clippers. There's money and connections to be had.

Of course, Columbus will always be an Ohio State town, and it should be. The Buckeyes will always rule. But with the rapid growth in Columbus—and with many of those new residents coming from areas where pro sports is just as popular as OSU football—there's room for a pro sports love.

Columbus has shown signs of directing that love to the Blue Jackets. Each of the previous playoff runs in franchise history was greeted by an outpouring of support. Playoff games in 2014, staged after Matt Calvert's OT goal provided the first postseason win in franchise history, were events. TV ratings jumped this year, and frankly you could argue a lesser city would have bid adieu to the Blue Jackets long ago considering the franchise's history of losing.

So what is Columbus, Ohio? Odds are, whatever answer you give now is somehow, some way related to the Blue Jackets.

And with another playoff run, my bet is, more and more, the answer is Columbus is a Jackets town.

Sitting Out the Anthem

*Reflections on the Columbus Blue Jackets,
Racism, and Protest*

DAN SKINNER

I don't really remember the first time I opted to not stand for the anthem in Nationwide Arena. In fact, I believe that it may have just been an omission, a moment during which I was responding to a text message or looking at team stats. In other words, I'm pretty sure the first time was not a consciously political act. After all, while I had long been conflicted about the presence of nationalist pomp and circumstance at sporting events, my story began before Colin Kaepernick was a household name and before Donald Trump called for firing football players who protest.

Here's the thing: I go to Columbus Blue Jackets games because I like hockey. I am a fan. I tolerate a lot of what happens in the arena—the advertisements of subpar products by villains of the working class like Papa John, the sexism of dressing "ice girls" in skimpy dresses while the men who clear the ice get to wear jumpsuits—because I love hockey. For some time I had successfully suspended my tendency to be political about everything (I'm a political scientist) to enjoy the game. In becoming a Blue Jackets season ticket holder I wanted something in my life that would just be . . . fun.

I do, however, remember the moment I realized that this was going to be harder than I thought it would.

Military Appreciation: An Everygame Affair

First, though, a bit of background. As has become customary for some years at American sporting events, the national anthem—"The Star-Spangled Banner"—is sung. If the Jackets are playing a Canadian team, the Canadian anthem, "Oh, Canada," is performed. Both versions are sung by the team's anthem singer, Leo Welsh, a local celebrity who sings in exchange for season tickets and a jersey. Leo is accompanied on the ice at each game by a guest—usually an Ohioan who is a member of the U.S. military or National Guard, though occasionally he is paired with a Boy Scout, an EMS worker, or something of that nature.

These game day rituals—officially known as "Military Salutes"—are brought to us (everything that happens in the arena is sponsored) by Elk & Elk, a local personal injury law firm. During the anthem, ticket scanners stop scanning tickets, creating a logjam of fans trying to enter the arena. Fans are asked to rise and (if applicable) remove their hats. Sometime during the first period, during a TV break, the arena (most of it, anyway) rises to recognize Leo's anthem guest, who is by now seated somewhere in the lower bowl of the arena. The result is 30–60 seconds of applause. This process is repeated at all 41 regular season home games, plus any post-season games, with which the Blue Jackets have had only limited success since their establishment in 2000.

But there's more. Though each game opens with military appreciation, there is also, at least once a year, a special "Military Appreciation Night." On Military Appreciation night, the stadium is adorned with red, white, and blue banners (made in China). The players do their pre-game warm ups in camouflaged jerseys. Essentially every moment without play, when they are not honoring a soldier, is filled with songs about how free and brave Americans are.

One saving grace of all this fanfare is that because hockey is an arena sport, there can be no Air Force flyovers as there are at Browns and Bengals football games. Because the arena is covered with ice, there can be no military marches or induction ceremonies like the ones that take place from time to time at Columbus Crew soccer games.

Having endured a few Military Appreciation nights in the past, in 2013 I decided that this time I would find a positive way to channel my energy. That day, before the game, I bought an 18" by 22" poster, and wrote on it, with a big Sharpie, "Hug a Social Worker." I arrived at the arena, however, only to be told after being flagged by a security guard that I would not be allowed to bring in my sign because it exceeded acceptable arena dimensions. I made my disappointment known and left the sign at the entrance . . . only to encounter, in my first moments in the arena, a person with a larger sign name-checking "the troops." It was clear: my sign was not denied entry not under the arena sign rules (22" x 28" or less), but the category of "Any other item deemed unacceptable by Nationwide Arena management." Pro-military censorship.

Never mind that social workers remain on the front line of addressing the epidemic of post-Bush-era post-traumatic stress disorder experienced by Iraq and Afghanistan veterans. These folks are all over Columbus and receive much of their care at Central Ohio's community health centers and VA facilities. Never mind that these civic heroes are a foundation of our schools and our hospitals, and are addressing the homeless crisis that continues to plague many Central Ohioans, including veterans. I started to see what I had long suspected, namely that supporting the troops at Nationwide Arena was not about a thoughtful respect for those who sacrifice for the nation. It had become a largely reflexive fetish.

It is perhaps here that my relationship with the anthem changed. I didn't stand for it. Or I sat it out, depending on your frame.

I guess I should have seen it coming. But I was surprised when this quiet act of resistance, born out of anger for the censoring of my sign, created a stir. People yelled at me. "Stand up!" The voices intensified: "Stand up, you asshole!" Fans behind me passive-aggressively talked among themselves, but in a voice that ensured that I would hear: "Can you believe this guy isn't standing?" "What the fuck is wrong with this guy?" They seethed, sneered, and stared. The irony was not lost on me: all of these songs of freedom were not license enough to allow me to sit quietly during a song.

What the Hell Is a Blue Jacket?

Without going too far down this nationalist rabbit hole, however, some context about the Blue Jackets might be helpful to appreciate the arena vibe. The team's name and imagery, after all, contains some explicitly political material. Many people assume that Native American connections are the origin of the team's name, since Blue Jacket was a famous Shawnee chief who lead the resistance against the white invasion of Shawnee lands that would eventually become Ohio (a word that itself means, roughly, "beautiful" in the Shawnee tongue). But, somewhat oddly, this is not the origin of the team's name. Instead, in line with the team's founder John H. McConnell's stated goal of acknowledging "patriotism, pride, and the rich Civil War history in the state of Ohio and city of Columbus," the Blue Jackets are billed as an homage to Ohio's role in the Civil War. As the team's official account explains, "Ohio contributed more of its population to the Union Army than any other state, while many of the Blue Coats worn by the Union soldiers were manufactured in Columbus." According to official lore, the team's name is actually the result of a "Name the Team" contest, held in conjunction with the Columbus-based fast food chain Wendy's, in which future fans submitted about 14,000 possible names. Ownership whittled it down to two: the Blue Jackets and the Justice—an inverse Sophie's Choice.

It is a unique feature of the team, in fact, that its thoroughgoing patriotism is reserved—at least in design—to the state and city levels. I'm not aware of another American professional sports team so enthralled with its own state-level political identity. As a consequence, however, very few people—locally as well as nationally—know what the team's name means. It remains the butt of many jokes among NHL hockey fans. You've got to give the management credit, though. Not only have they opted to not go in, as others have, on racist cultural appropriations of Native Americans (one need only look to that racist baseball team to the north for that), a move that would be gutsy considering that the Shawnee were marched Westward, many of them slaughtered, leaving only the name of the state itself for us to remember. Instead, they put together perhaps the nation's most inscrutable mascot, a green bee with a blue jacket named Stinger—the "Bug with an Attitude"—who is presumably green because that's what happens when you put a blue jacket on a yellow bee. Hey, at least it's not racist.

This is all to say that I understand that the Blue Jackets are a team with a patriotic theme. It is also, as I've noted, a somewhat interesting kind of patriotism, rooted in a Civil War history that I largely support, especially as part of my own anti-racist, abolitionist politics. And I admit it: I think it's kind of cool that there is a Civil War-style cannon in the arena. I love that it annoys visiting teams when it goes off.

A New Norm

Though I've provided it as context, these associations and this history are beside the point. The anthem that has been forced on fans at every game in the U.S. is part of a mandatory pro-war politics that has been turbocharged since 9/11. When attacks at the hands of terrorists occur, the anthem in Nationwide Arena is often followed up with chants of "USA, USA." While most of these moments are clearly assumed to be in reference to attacks on "us" by "them," the chant also occurs at moments when our country, in my view, has little to be proud of, as when lax gun laws allow a madman to shoot hundreds of country music fans in Las Vegas or on the anniversary of the Sandy Hook shootings that left 20 kids dead. The killing of Trayvon Martin, of course, spawned the Black Lives Matter movement (which was at the time given a strong voice by Akron native Lebron James, at that time on hiatus with the Miami Heat before his return to Cleveland). The 2014 killing of 12-year old Tamir Rice by Cleveland police received not a mention in the arena. Nor is the deep racism in Columbus—from its skyrocketing black infant mortality rate (second in the nation) to its rampant real estate discrimination and segregated schools, to the killings of 13-year-old Tyre King and 23-year-old Timothy Davis in 2016—ever pondered. In most ways, Nationwide Arena is an echo chamber of an uncritical nationalist bias that takes a clear and racialized perspective on worthy and unworthy killings. It is a microcosm of American society itself.

My decision to sit out the anthem had not yet linked up with these protest movements. 2013 preceded the present national moment. After Military Appreciation night that year, however, when I was yelled at, I came to realize that not only had my act of sitting become a political statement, but so was standing. There was no neutral place. To stand was to capitulate. I was caught in between.

But if these were all preliminary stirrings, the next game clarified things for me. While sitting through the anthem, I was tapped on the shoulder: "Stand the hell up." My guest for that game started to talk back to—ok, yell at—this person, but I pulled them back. My decision to sit was mine alone. If these fans want to argue with me, that's fine. But I'm not going to yell back. Let them be bothered.

The next game things got worse. While sitting I started to feel things landing on my head. Fans a few rows back were throwing popcorn. I looked over to my left and caught the gaze of my usher, a senior citizen and military veteran, but he looked the other way. I approached the usher during the intermission and, when I asked him whether he was going to say something to these people, he responded: "You have to stand. It's the law." Well, of course, it is decidedly not the law. Shocked, I stated the obvious: "Well, that's absurd. But it is your job to protect the people in your section. I hope you'll say something." He did, but I watched him deliver the orders softly, with a kind of clear solidarity that made it clear that he was on their side.

Though I have literally dozens of stories of this kind, I will share just one more, since it encapsulates so much of the larger story. Several games later, while sitting for the anthem, I felt the stare of the people next to me—a father and daughter. The anthem ended, the puck dropped, and within seconds the Jackets scored a goal. I immediately jumped to my feet in celebration, as I often do, seeing as I was at a hockey game and all. The man then turned to me and said, "So, you'll cheer for a goal, but not a soldier?" Since they asked a question, I answered honestly: "Yup. I paid for a ticket to a hockey game, not a patriotic celebration." The woman muttered: "You're disgusting, unbelievable . . ." I felt their gaze for the remainder of the game. They seethed. I'm not sure they even watched the game.

In a way, this vignette captures my thinking on these moments. I no more want my sports entwined with nationalism than I do religion. And while the Blue Jackets can do whatever they want in programming their event, which is, after all, entertainment, I am there for the main show—the game.

Finally, a comment on my guests. I bring lots of different people to Blue Jackets games: family, friends, colleagues, former students, and friends of friends. As testament to the arena vibe, more than one female guest I have brought to games has told me that they would like to sit out the anthem with me, but do not feel safe doing so. This is doubly true for non-white friends. I always make sure that my guests know that I do not care whether they stand or sit and that what I do in no way should be read as my preference about what they do. In fact, as I explain below, I often do stand, especially when I feel something particular about the person being honored (such as the rare first responder or pediatric cancer patient). Sometimes, when I feel strongly that my nation did something good that week—like establish marriage equality—I stand. The day after Donald Trump was elected, I sat. I've been sitting a lot since that election.

Anthems, Protests, and Hockey

Former 49ers quarterback Colin Kaepernick's courageous actions of course brought new context to all of this. In 2018, what one does during the anthem is a response to a political moment. There is no way around it. Here again, however, just a bit more history is helpful for understanding what is happening in Nationwide Arena.

The anthem, readers may know, only came to be played routinely at sporting events during World War II. At this time, players rarely came out for the performance. It was, in other words, a fairly organic and reactive occurrence, a response to a temporary national mobilization, marked by a congressional war declaration. After World War II ended, however, NFL commissioner Elmer Layden declared that "The playing of the national anthem should be as much a part of every game as the kickoff." He added: "We must not drop it simply because the war is over. We should never forget what it stands for."

It is here, perhaps, that my core problem with the anthem as a sporting event ritual becomes clear. NHL hockey teams play 82 regular season games. That's a lot of games and a lot of nationalism. (I tend to agree with former Cubs owner Philip K. Wrigley, who refused to play the anthem at every game because he believed that doing so cheapened the song.) The anthem, as the NFL's Layden noted at the time, was linked to support for the nation during war. The problem is that today, it seems that we are always at war. Or actually, there's another, more serious problem: the United States has not actually declared war since World War II. What we have today are a constant stream of unauthorized military actions—in Libya, Yemen, Syria, and beyond—that have become a backdrop to

American life itself. In other words, the "you must stand" of Nationwide Arena is linked to an uncritical and permanent war posture that is part and parcel of a larger American class warfare to the extent that it is being bankrolled by the American working class including, undoubtedly, many Columbus Blue Jackets fans. We have forgotten what it means to be at war, and to be a nation of sacrifice, just as the wash of the anthem's daily appearance has become rote and automatic—stand up, sit down—instead of meaningful.

Within the national conversation that arose in 2016, when Kaepernick began his movement, the Blue Jackets were not just any team. They had by that point brought on board a nationally known coach, John Tortorella, a coach with a Stanley Cup ring, but also something of a hothead (sometimes for ill, sometimes for good, from a sports perspective). Tortorella, who was also slated to coach the U.S. World Team, made national headlines with his comments about his players and the anthem, telling *Sports Illustrated*, "If any of my players sit on the bench for the national anthem, they will sit there the rest of the game." His comments about the anthem were also motivated by the fact that his son has served multiple tours in Afghanistan as part of the U.S. Army Special Forces. Tortorella has spoken often about how hockey is just a game, and that soldiers like his son are infinitely more praiseworthy than hockey players, who are, at the end of the day, entertainers. I think it's more complicated than that. There is too much taking place right outside the arena's doors for the question to be reduced to one of "supporting the troops" or not.

There's also a matter of players' rights. As president of the National Hockey League Players Association (NHPLA), Donald Fehr noted at the time, "We believe each player may choose to speak out or engage in peaceful protest on matters that are important to him. A player is entitled to his own views on political and social issues, and the right of each player to express such views deserves respect. Should a Player decide to make such a peaceful protest, he would of course have the full support of the NHLPA in regard to his right to do so."

Now, I tend to take workers' rights seriously, and I appreciate unions. After all, as readers should recall, Ohio is not only a state with a deep Civil War history, but Columbus is the home of the American Federation of Labor, founded in 1886—it is historically a union town. Unions aside, however, there is a difference between what a coach can tell a player to do and what an arena can tell a paying customer to do. While the arena has rules about the conduct of fans (especially the use of profanity and disorderly conduct), it can hardly be stretched to sitting out the anthem. One unique thing about being in Nationwide Arena—and many other arenas around the country as well—is that there appears to be an assumption that we are all similarly obligated. There has been a merging and misunderstanding of what is mandated by law, what is expected by social norms, and what is a smart business decision (and the NHL is, at base, a business). What bugs me is that few people seem to recognize the inherent contradiction in their moans and groans when I sit, namely that they are behaving fascistically themselves, and undoing the very freedom about which they sing in the process.

Going into the 2017 season, there were rumblings that all-star forward, Joel Ward—a black Canadian player now with the Sharks—might take a knee. While that has not come to pass (and I don't begrudge Ward the decision), we got a glimpse of what might happen had he done so through when J. T. Brown, an African American forward on the Tampa Bay Lightning, raised his fist in protest at the end of the anthem. Brown was described by some in the Tampa media as, among other things, a "troublemaker" and "privileged athlete showing ungratefulness." Brown received death threats for his act and only lukewarm support from his teammates.

Hockey, Race, and the Politics of Protest

To state the obvious, NHL hockey is a sport dominated by white men, with fewer than 30 African American players (or players of African descent) out of hundreds of roster positions.

Unlike the NFL and NBA, sports in which a strong majority of the players are African American, the vast majority of hockey players are white and 75% hail from countries outside of the U.S. I'm guessing that most are not eager to get involved in American politics. At the same time, the whiteness of the sport produces a different dynamic than one gets in the NBA and NFL. For example, Boston Bruins fans tweeted racist epithets after Ward (then with the Capitals') scored a game-winning goal against the Bruins in the 2012 playoffs, and when former Canadiens' defenseman P. K. Subban scored one against them in the 2014 playoffs. Ward, Subban, Wayne Simmonds of the Philadelphia Flyers, and Washington's Devante Smith-Pelly have all reported being subjected to racist comments by fans and being isolated on the basis of the color of their skin.

The addition of Seth Jones—an amazingly talented young defenseman and an African American—to the Blue Jackets defensive corps has not only given the team depth and skill, but it has had a visible impact on the fans as well. I do not know Jones's position on the matter of anthem protests, police violence against African Americans, or Black Lives Matter. I only know that were he to mount a protest, the likely rejection of Jones's voice—and hopefully those who would stand with him—would be swift and unsupportive.

To be fair, the Blue Jackets organization has made some strides in terms of negotiating the racial representation of the sport being played on the ice. I know several African Americans in Columbus for whom Jones's signing made a big difference. There appear to be more African Americans attending games. The jumbotron camera operator is clearly engaging in an attempt to put a more diverse picture on the screen, as well, even if those faces are not quite representative of the greater whole. Representation matters.

Sitting It Out in the Age of Trump

Especially considering the current political temperature, I wouldn't expect the people of Columbus to take my sitting for the anthem without complaint. I'm sure I'd receive a similar reception at Madison Square Garden in New York or PNC Arena in Raleigh. I don't mind that. I know that the U.S. is a country that rallies around the troops and little else. I know that Ohio is home to several military bases—especially Wright-Patterson Air Force Base, where most of the Blue Jackets' Military Salute honorees serve. I also recognize that those who are honored are probably hardworking people who deserve to be treated with respect. In fact, I do treat them with respect when I interact with them, not as soldiers, but as fellow human beings and hockey fans.

But all this is beside the point.

I hope that in sitting I can contribute, in some insignificant way, to making Nationwide Arena a more thoughtful place where we can not only display our nationalism, but we can find ways to care more for all Ohioans. I'd like to have more productive and reciprocal conversations with my fellow Blue Jackets fans about the tone of the space in which we spend (depending on overtime and playoff games) 102.5 hours together each season. For my first few years as a Blue Jackets fan, I sat next to a Navy veteran who respected my decision to sit, and told me that my right to do so was one of the reasons he served. We had wonderful conversations during the games. Contrast this with my usher's ill-informed views, and you've got the makings of a good conversation.

I close with an admission, however. As with many of the ongoing challenges that have come to a head during the Trump years, I am tired of sitting for the anthem. I never knew that sitting could take so much energy. I'm also frankly not sure that it's worth it. So these days, I often show up later than I used to in the hopes of missing it. If I arrive on time, I use the anthem as an opportunity to get a beer or use the bathroom. The world of commerce, bustling just beyond the arena seats, pays no mind to the song being sung inside. Plumbing flows and then the puck drops.

In a City Marked by Change, Columbus Crew SC Remains a Powerful, Unifying Force

HANIF ABDURRAQIB

In the beginning of Columbus Crew SC, there was no MAP-FRE Stadium. There was no Nordecke; there were no chants of "Glory to Columbus" rattling the city's night sky.

In fact, Crew SC reflects the city that it was born in, most notably in how much it has changed over the years.

But on the team's first spring game night in 1996, on the field at Ohio State's Ohio Stadium, there were the staple colors, black and gold. There was the city's first professional sports star, Brian McBride, ripping up and down the pitch during a 4–0 thrashing of soon-to-be rivals DC United. There was a college football city, starved for professional sports, watching this new game played in the Buckeyes' mecca.

And most memorably, as I noted that day from the crowd, there were flags: American flags, the flag of Columbus, and those of a host of other nations. The flag of Ghana waved high in the nosebleed seats. A group right below where I stood waved the Jamaican flag. In a section to our right, a small group of children, close to my age at the time, held the Somali flag in their hands, beaming.

The team's come a long way since then—up to hosting the 2015 MLS Cup Final this Sunday, Dec. 6. All those years of change reflect change in the city itself.

When discussing Crew SC's importance to Columbus, it is necessary to first understand Columbus, the city in which I've spent most of my life. Columbus is quintessentially Midwestern, in layout, population temperament, and ice cream selection. It will never be New York or Los Angeles, but that doesn't mean that it won't keep occasionally trying to compete, sometimes at the cost of its own communities. At the same time, Columbus has almost always been a place where those who have been displaced—by urgent desire or by circumstances beyond their control—can resettle and find comfort.

Crew SC came along at an important time for the city. In 1995, Columbus welcomed a large number of Somali refugees, drawn to it by its cost of living, plentiful jobs for multilingual adults, and welfare programs headed up by the Somali Community Association of Ohio, which helped refugees with recovery from Somalia's civil war.

Today, Columbus boasts the second-largest Somali population in the U.S., many on the city's Northside. Around this time, the number of Ghanaian immigrants in Columbus also rose, creating a culture shift in the heart of Columbus, especially among youth, many of whom were assimilating into new schools and looking for new outputs for energy and pride.

Cliché as it may be, soccer remains a universal language. So in 1999, when Crew SC got its own stadium, it stood as a central meeting point for these converging communities, where all the contents of Columbus's melting pot could be poured out and blended together. And now, in a city marked by development, gentrification, and flux, it remains one of the most reliable places for this to continue.

The stands still fill with people from every corner of a city that, because of these forces, pulls them further and further away from each other every year. The Hudson Street Hooligans chant while La Turbina Amarilla plays their bass and snare drums along with the chants. Flags of nations still blanket the stadium—Mexico, Ethiopia, Sierra Leone, Ghana, and still, of course, Somalia. When the game ends, everyone drives to their respective parts of the city. Some people drive past places they can no longer afford; some people drive to expensive apartment buildings that replaced the lower-income housing that stood there before. There is no way to romanticize how a city can eat its own, and who it leaves behind in the process.

But Crew SC, for nearly two decades now, has provided a source of pride and unity. A home game is a place where you can come and see yourself reflected both on the field and in the stands, whether your parents escaped a country embroiled in civil war, or if you're simply escaping your parents in the suburbs for the night.

When people doubt the power of North American soccer, I imagine they have never walked outside of MAPFRE Stadium at halftime of a game and seen young Somali kids on the mini-pitch, dazzling the kids from the suburban select teams with their footwork and energy. I imagine they've never seen a child's eyes light up with the realization of what is possible when Wil Trapp, a product of a Columbus suburb mere miles from the stadium, takes the field in the city where he was raised.

They've probably never seen the eyes of a Ghanaian while Harrison Afful tears along the edges of the field, defending and attacking with reckless abandon. I imagine they've probably also never tried to make their way through the parking lot after a Crew SC victory, before giving up, getting out of their car, and chanting and singing along with whatever supporters are left, stretching their joy for as long as possible. These things, all of them, matter a great deal. The game is a beautiful game, indeed, and its meaning goes well beyond the game itself.

Late in leg two of this year's 2015 Audi MLS Cup Eastern Conference Semifinal, with the series tied 3–3 on the aggregate, I had resigned myself to hoping for penalty kicks. And then, the team's fortunes changed in an instant.

With only a few minutes left in extra time, beloved Crew SC star Kei Kamara, a refugee who escaped war in Sierra Leone with his family at 16, took a cross from Congolese left winger Cedrick Mabwati and headed home the game-winning goal.

It was a moment that will, without question, go down as one of Columbus's greatest sports moments. And Kamara sprinted to MAPFRE's north corner, stood tall, and bathed in the gold and black. It was clear, then, that the most important thing about Crew SC has never changed. As conflicting forces push and pull on the city I live in, unsure of what it wants to become, the team is an important thing that still unites.

The City That Raised Me Has a New Face

TIFFANY WILLIAMS

It's an odd thing: to be both distant and present.

Growing up, we called the King-Lincoln Bronzeville, simply, Mt. Vernon. It was home to the infamous "Coming Home" festival where all the black people gathered with loud music, doing the electric slide up and down Mt. Vernon Ave., gracefully rolling their bodies—cool as a fan on humid summer days. Though I grew up in North Linden, Mt. Vernon was not foreign to me. My elementary school was just a half mile from the King Arts Complex. The activity bus would pick me up some weeknights from Duxberry Park and head to the center where I had keyboard lessons. She was a short, spirited woman, my keyboard teacher. She had long straight black hair, an inviting smile, and a fiery spirit that always made me want to try again when my fingers slipped and hit the incorrect keys.

Duxberry Park was where I first heard the names Aminah Robinson and Elijah Pierce. I studied their art with regular field trips to the Wexner Center for the Arts and the Columbus Main Library. There, I was also introduced to Langston Hughes, sang with Arnett Howard, and folk danced with Mimi Chenfeld. It was an eclectic place where arts was appreciated, respected, and cultivated. It was where I learned I wanted to be a writer. Since then I have wanted to be nothing else, nothing more.

In middle school, my education landed me closer to my neighborhood at the now closed Linmoor Middle School. It was perfectly nestled between Hamilton Elementary School and Linden-McKinley High School, allowing the neighborhood kids to live and learn together, should their parents so choose. People would frown when I told them I attended Linmoor, more than likely because its landscape was South Linden and their minds immediately thought of the crime, gangs, and any other negative idiosyncrasy they could come up with to assume I was underprivileged. Still, I thrived there. I walked home from school with my older brother and then, when he entered high school, with my friends who lived within two miles from me. Linmoor holds some of my fondest memories as a child. Fights broke out in school, and after school, we were threatened with Zero Tolerance; classes were rowdy, and sometimes the teachers couldn't get control of the classroom. But we laughed a lot, I read the *Autobiography of Malcolm X* for the first time, played basketball, bonded with teachers, attended hotel parties with friends, and passed notes with boys.

I know now that my introduction to Otterbein College through Linmoor was a community service project by its students and that I was probably a statistic due to my family size, income, and targeted neighborhood. Through the Linmoor-Otterbein Mentoring Program I saw a college campus for the first time, experienced overnight living in a dorm room, and saw a picture of what life could be like outside of my neighborhood's boundaries. It was a paradigm shift. Their community service project turned into an opportunity for me to earn a scholarship, as long as my grades were at or above a 3.0 in high school. I kept my end of the deal and Otterbein kept theirs: I graduated with a bachelor's of art in Journalism in 2005.

I'm not sure where or when I learned to flee from the same inner city neighborhood that raised me. I think it was de facto living; that as an African American, once you became a member of the middle class, you should move up and out. It is what I assumed I would do; no one explicitly told me to do so. I was to be happy about doing it, never thinking about the alternatives; never thinking of what would become of my neighborhood, my peers, or their families who chose to stay—or, who did not have the choice.

It was my husband, Keith, who suggested our freshly blended family move to King-Lincoln in 2013. We'd followed the expected path, living in Pickerington the first year of our marriage. I looked at him sideways, the same way people looked at me when I told them what school I attended or at Otterbein when I introduced myself in class and announced the high school and neighborhood I was from. I had fallen victim too, I realized. I had internalized the television's perception of violence, blamed the residents who were still there, and unapologetically turned my nose up to the thought of building a life there. But the memories danced in my mind and replayed over and over again. I never personally identified with a negative experience in the area. It was the perception of the area that drove my fears and anxiety. When I realized fear was driving my decision, there was nothing left. The memories of those noted above were tangible experiences before the apprehension of others began to take over. All happy and concrete memories that were a far cry from the crime infested, underemployed, unemployed, and poverty-stricken narrative that made its way to local news broadcasts and came to the forefront of my psyche without me understanding they had made a home there. The dancing in my mind eventually matched my husband's persuasion fueled by his passion for work in the area. We settled into our home in August 2014, just south of Mt. Vernon AME, next to a community garden with a perfect view of the destruction of Poindexter Village.

Today, the demographics are becoming more fuzzy, the architecture more modern, the gentrification more apparent. In the early months of us living in our home, one of my neighbors, a middle-aged white man, was walking his large dog, calmly, down Mt. Vernon Ave. one morning. My face scrunched as I looked at my husband as we were passing in our vehicle; his face matching mine. We burst into laughter at the oddity of such a sight. "Doesn't he know this is Mt. Vernon?" I said out loud, a rhetorical question that felt necessary to give breath.

We laughed at the absurdity of a well-dressed white man comfortably walking his dog in one of the city's most undesirable neighborhoods. Although we laughed, we knew the seriousness in my question and in our expressions. I understand, more now as I live and raise my children in a neighborhood not too far off from my own growing up, that the same messaging can deter and detract while also advance and elevate.

Perhaps if I lived outside of 270, I'd nod my head in agreement or silently applaud when Columbus makes yet another "Top 10" of this or that list, that denotes its ability to thrive through school systems, diverse modes of transportation, professional pursuits, and growing industries in tech. Juxtapose that against driving down Long Street or Monroe or 18th Street and seeing abandoned homes and businesses, countless liquor stores in a half-mile radius; and let's not forget the high infant mortality rate that's ranked #1 in my very own zip code. And what of those displaced residents of Poindexter Village, forced to leave the very place that housed their families for generations? Can they find home in the vouchers provided? Can they find solace in returning to a neighborhood they know but do not recognize? Should I praise those lists? Normally, I read and reread in confusion I'm hoping will turn into enlightenment about the Columbus I want to experience but do not see myself in. I want more faces who look melanated like mine where the best schools are housed and where the perceptions of the safest neighborhoods reside. I want to live respectably in the city of my birth where I can celebrate my culture freely and my white counterparts won't feel threatened because of loud music in cars or raised voices on porch stoops. I don't want to live, work, attend school outside of 270 in order to gain those attributes imagined in the American Dream while also giving up my culture, sense of community, and pride in familial traditions. Can I have both? Can Columbus have both?

Gone are the days of activity buses that transported children safely from school to community centers. There are no after school classes offered at King Arts Complex. Linmoor Middle School is closed, as is my high school, Brookhaven High School. Coming Home is just a blurred memory in my mind fused with reminiscent lines from my peers or elders that miss how it "used to be." My grandmother, 81, speaks fondly of her childhood growing up in King-Lincoln Bronzeville. Back then, they called it, simply, Bronzeville. Her childhood home on McCoy Street no longer stands—demolished by freeway construction on what is now the campus of Fort Hayes Metropolitan High School. Afterward, they moved to N. Garfield Avenue. She talks of walking to the also demolished Carl Brown IGA to get the family's groceries, her large porch that housed many conversations between her and her six siblings, including five girls. It is the whisper of these memories that play and replay in my ear when I walk down Mt. Vernon or feel a wave of hesitation meet me in the very neighborhood I live. The footsteps of my people, my family, walked the same roads with celebration and freedom.

This is my hope for Columbus: that Black and Brown people are afforded the same opportunities to live the same quality of life as every other group; where the neighborhoods we live in are not ignored only to be praised when real estate development and money is the prize; to make priority access to resources; to face crime as a by-product of poverty and not a disease because of my race. Ultimately, to not have my children repeat the same experiences in the city of their birth that I once did; to change the narrative and build a path of least resistance. I'm keeping hope alive.

What Would Jane Say?

SARAH MARSOM

Wrapping around downtown Columbus is a gaping wound—
a wound that refuses to heal properly, caused by urban re-
newal and known to residents and travelers as I-70/71,
OH-315, and I-670. After World War II, cities across the United
States saw an influx of population and wealth. Columbus wel-
comed new industries, such as the Lustron Corporation, and
the development of new neighborhoods: Grandview Heights,
Bexley, and Clintonville.

The allure of "new" led city planners to wonder what to
do with the older neighborhoods. Downtown neighborhoods
in many communities were in decline. It was a combination
of population loss, as people migrated to the new urban sub-
urbs, and the Great Depression, which had resulted in a lack
of maintenance. People who had the financial means left the
city for their American dream: a house with a yard and a white
picket fence. Many city planners believed the best response
was urban renewal. Urban renewal was the demolition of
areas that the city believed would benefit best from being rede-
veloped. In many cases, the redevelopment was the creation of
modern road systems, but the development also could include
the construction of new modern structures.

Urban renewal is also called "slum clearance" because of the strategy predominantly targeting individuals of a lower socioeconomic level. Immigrant and African American neighborhoods were also targeted in the name of city advancement and redevelopment. One hero emerged in this time of destruction: Jane Jacobs. Born and raised in Scranton, Pennsylvania, Jacobs moved to New York City when she was 19, in 1935, with the dream of being a writer. By 1952, she was writing for *Architectural Forum* and visiting construction sites across the country. This role advanced her understanding of the built environment and its impact on community. Jacobs developed a belief that the city exists for the people.

Her work influenced her personal crusade to save her neighborhood, Greenwich Village, from demolition. New York City's city planner, Robert Moses, intended to demolish several blocks and displace 1,000 businesses and 132 homes, in addition to modifying Washington Square Park to be a major thoroughfare (1949). Greenwich Village, at this time, was comprised of families, immigrants, and small businesses. Jacobs and her family renovated their personal dwelling. They believed Moses's plan would be detrimental to residential life. Through vocal advocacy at city meetings and public protest, Jacobs and other activists were able to dissuade the government from proceeding with the destruction of their neighborhood.

Greenwich Village led to a career in activism for Jacobs; she fought against Moses's plan to demolish Little Italy in New York City for an expressway in the 1960s. When she moved to Toronto, she was a vocal advocate against yet another proposed expressway that would eliminate residential areas. Her involvement in Greenwich Village led to her writing *The Death and Life of Great American Cities,* which was published in 1961, and would shape future generations of urbanists. Her writing advocates against urban renewal and proposes that neighborhoods should have both newer and older architecture. In addition, these neighborhoods should optimize their potential walkability by providing mixed uses. Jacobs wrote other books, such as *The Economy of Cities* (1969) and *Cities and the*

Wealth of Nations (1985), but this work would be her crown jewel.

Jacobs passed away in 2006, but her legacy continues to grow. Ten years after her death, the Tiny Jane Project was founded. Small dolls are created in the image of Jane Jacobs in an effort to educate youth about urban planning and historic preservation. Every doll sold supports a conference scholarship fund, which supports young preservationists. The Tiny Jane Project emerged from a desire to educate others on why places of the past matter and how these places can be incorporated into contemporary communities.

Those who hold Columbus near and dear to their hearts know that we could benefit from the help that Jacobs once gave New York and Toronto. Luckily for us, I've spent the last year with Tiny Jane. Tiny Jane has many opinions on the Columbus of the past and the Columbus of today, but the past must be examined in order for her to recommend tactics for urban renewal healing.

Columbus's wound is the remnant of the city's urban renewal efforts, and neighborhoods are still being impacted today. When neighborhood residents left their urban neighborhoods for newly developed suburbs such as Grandview Heights or Bexley, the departure had an adverse effect on the original settlements of Columbus. In German Village, the top third of the neighborhood was demolished to make room for I-70/71. Much of the neighborhood, then known as the South End, was neglected due to the loss of residents whose German heritage had led to discrimination in World War I and the same residents losing their jobs during prohibition. Older neighborhood residents tell stories of gangsters shooting opponents during a game of poker at a local establishment or chickens walking down the streets. They talk of the neighborhood gardens and of the effort to preserve the neighborhood after the interstate destroyed much of its history.

The efforts of Frank Fetch to organize and to activate the community prevented further destruction. Fetch, a city employee, understood that legislation would be necessary to protect the community's remaining historic assets. In 1960, Fetch, alongside numerous neighborhood residents, founded the German Village Society: a neighborhood nonprofit to advocate for the preservation of the neighborhood's built environment. That same year, the residents were successful at lobbying the newly minted German Village to be the city's first historic district, one of the first locally designated historic areas in the country.

On the east side of Columbus, the Bronzeville neighborhood suffered the same fate of housing demolition for the western portion of the neighborhood to create I-71. Bronzeville was the heart of the African American community in Columbus by the early 1900s. Unlike German Village, the neighborhood did not have a champion to prevent the further destruction; neither did the neighborhoods north of downtown Columbus, which were disconnected from downtown with the construction of I-670.

Looking at these communities today, one can see the difference between a neighborhood that had a champion and the neighborhoods that have struggled to reclaim their damaged identity. After the demolition of a portion of Bronzeville, the neighborhood was frequently called the Near East Side, with different areas retaining their historic area names. The renaming of Bronzeville to be King-Lincoln in 2002, to make the neighborhood more marketable to developers, illustrates the city's inability to understand how to heal the urban renewal wound. In response to crime in Italian and Victorian Village north of downtown Columbus, and in an effort to connect the High Street commercial corridor revitalization downtown, the city of Columbus partnered with the Ohio Department of Transportation and private developers to create a cap, a bridge that allowed for businesses to be constructed to hide the view of I-670. The cap, which opened in 2004, is a Band-Aid to help heal a specific area.

Tiny Jane believes that understanding the history of a neighborhood can assist in reactivating its vibrancy and allow holistic redevelopment. While German Village was able to mitigate additional damage to the neighborhood by acquiring historic district designation, its adjacent neighborhoods directly east were also negatively impacted by the interstate, and the somewhat arbitrary boundaries determined by advocates in the 1960s led to organic redevelopment. The City of Columbus has made efforts to empower these neighborhoods and Bronzeville/King-Lincoln through the creation of the area commissions and by allowing residents to have a voice in demolition and zoning variances, but still the power ultimately lies with the city regarding demolition.

Both Italian and Victorian Village respectively became locally designated historic districts in 1973. A historic designation is not necessarily the solution to all urban renewal wounds. However, it can slow the demolition that continues to negatively affect neighborhoods like Bronzeville impacted by the slum clearance of the mid-20th century. The local designation also implies that certain stories of history are a higher priority to preserve.

When looking for ways to mend this wound, Tiny Jane would encourage a demolition moratorium in the undesignated areas until there is an understanding of what historic assets remain. Removing a structure continues to perpetuate the urban renewal belief that elimination of a structure eliminates the cause of a perceived issue. The City of Columbus needs to listen to what neighborhood residents want and need when making decisions for zoning, demolition, and new development. Contemporary structures can be integrated into these damaged historic areas to cultivate people with diverse housing wishes. These historic areas need to remain designated as mixed-use commercial and residential to encourage a walkable neighborhood. These are some of the aspects of these neighborhoods that existed when they were first developed that make them desirable today. German Village, Italian Village, and Victorian Village are considered some of the most desirable neighborhoods in Columbus.

So, why is Bronzeville/King-Lincoln still struggling with vacancy and neglected properties? In part, because Columbus refuses to acknowledge its existing residents' wishes and thought it was best to rebrand with a new name. A new name, while it pays homage to African American history, ignores the site-specific history. Identity is integral to the rebuilding of a community. Italian, Victorian, and German Village were all able to create their identities during the time of crisis and creation of the interstate. Bronzeville is seeing a rise in advocacy, but where is the city support? Tiny Jane challenges the neighborhood residents and advocates to change the city's perspective and hold them to a higher standard. Bronzeville's history deserves to be preserved beyond art panels over the I-70 overpass.

It is not too late for Columbus to heal old wounds. Channel your inner Jane Jacobs and advocate for your neighborhood. Even the tiniest action can make a difference.

Where the Sidewalk Ends

STACY JANE GROVER

It was Saint Patrick's Day at Bernie's. I was fifteen in a dress for the first time publicly and happening upon this throng of bodies churning bacchanal underground. I lingered, a phantom creeping below the stairs, in order to come to my senses. Slowly, over the guitars, the reverb, the increasing tempo, I could hear the voices shouting in unison, "Why we drink when we're told not to/I guess that's just what we're born to do."

I was greeted with a touch on the elbow, a smile, a look, and the stranger shouted, "Fuck yeah, lady, fuck yeah." The first time I wore a dress in public, in a room full of strangers, was the first time I was affirmed. What I feared was just a celebration of the spectacle of me turned out to be a genuine welcome, a peculiar invitation to return. And return I did.

Traveling to that place became a pilgrimage that led to other places.

To the Short North, the land behind the long dark stretch between 7th and 2nd. I was taken to the Chamber and the Garden where I met other queer people like me, other people that looked like me, people who allowed me to see that a future existed, that adult and trans* and queer went together and made for a potent, liberating mix.

To Magnolia's where the stone bench used to sit. I'd run my fingers over the names scribbled in sharpie, indicators of past lives screaming, "*I was here.*" I talked to strangers on that bench. I met the woman who called it home. I felt the weight of the city that night, its expansiveness. The moonlight shining above the power lines and chimneys in the damp evening air of spring left me momentarily breathless.

To the High Five, to the exhilaration walking from the abandoned gas station across the street at night. I found sanctuary in that place, a community I lost and have never fully recovered. To Old North, the welcome refuge of shops and bars dark and chaotic enough for me to be invisible in.

To Clintonville, to the resale store where another trans woman helped me find dresses that fit my shoulders, my unique shape, and shoes that would make my feet look smaller. Transmitted there between her fingers and the edges of the hair she pulled back for me was a knowing, a wisdom, that it does get better. But nothing gets better.

Three miles of High Street seemed bigger than any of the fields in which I grew up, longer than any winding country road that led somewhere else, but nowhere, really.

The skyscrapers looked like black charred weed stalks on the horizon, like when a bonfire envelops the grass and field in the careless tired haze of August nights when beer and humidity have eroded your senses. You wake up and see it through the thick dew on the grass in the morning. On the overlook in Chestnut Ridge, that is what Columbus looks like through the canopy. The buildings give off a radiant reflected light. Watchtowers, guardians, beacons. The city was these things and more to many of us from the small towns dotting the Southeast in the forgotten hinterlands between Columbus and Athens. It was the nearest "real city," the nearest "big" city, as we called it. US-33 became a lifeline to those things that are slow to percolate rural areas. The material things, objects to which we attach meaning. Objects that spark memory and give us a framework for now, for the future. There was the music, art, and fashion. And then there were the social things like acceptance, validation, and family. The space to explore identity, the confidence to come back and try things, to create a reality that wasn't yet real, to concoct from the disparate fragments of things glimpsed a world unto our own. It is through the material that the world gains social meaning, and the material is made present by the social. We saw what we wanted and recreated a distinctly local form of it.

The city that revealed itself to me in small, quiet, sacred moments, has been in constant flux. The Columbus I found myself in a wandering stranger, a dysphoric transgender vagabond, no longer exists. The physical traces of that time have and will continue to disappear beneath new multi-story mixed-use buildings, paved over into parking lots, moved to the outskirts of town to make way for something better, something newer.

A new Target and luxury condominiums will fill the empty hole where Bernie's used to be. The Chamber has closed. The Garden and Magnolia's remain, two guard lions flanking the sides of High Street in what may be one of the few remaining blocks of the Short North of my memory. The stone bench has been removed. The woman who used to live there died. The High Five is now a trendy taco restaurant. Hipsters have devoured the resale shop in Clintonville.

Now Columbus feels small, smaller than any field or winding country road that leads somewhere else, but nowhere, really. The forced relocation of great communities and the inevitable closing of welcoming spaces took with it the feeling of belonging.

The empty gas station on 5th became a business from which I was fired after calling out harassment from coworkers. The Short North became a place of violence. One night, outside the Stonewall Center, the sidewalk a kaleidoscopic sea, three men in a drunken haze tried to rob me. Again, the next day in the full glory of noontime, a man tried to assault me outside the liquor store. Even within *my* community and its spaces, I was unable to find room to breathe. Transgender groups became unwelcoming after criticism. Queer groups turned insular and exclusive. Finally, the brutal arrests of four black protestors at the Pride parade signaled that even the ragged tethers that bind the letters *LGBT* together often seem un-mendable. Some things get better. Nothing gets better.

What does remain as indicators of the city I remember are its sidewalks. The famed architect Louis Sullivan and his contemporaries conceived of skyscrapers as having a base, a middle, and a crown. Pedestrians were meant to interact with the first two stories. The long middle was plain and led the eyes up to the decorated crown. This design was intended to mitigate scale, but cities kept growing up. Most buildings became the size that skyscrapers were in Sullivan's time. When the whole field of view is tall, looking up becomes unmanageable.

With the pervasiveness of smartphones and other devices, pedestrians are looking down while walking through cities. Magazines and newspapers tell us to look up, to see the wonder of the architecture left to us from the past. But looking up disorients me. I look down.

Trans* individuals are used to looking down when we walk, to not make eye contact, to not provoke, to be invisible in a place where what we want most is visibility. The Columbus of my awakening is now a Columbus of sidewalks. "What people are within, the building is without," Sullivan is noted for having said. But I am no longer within these buildings. So I find the small spaces.

Under the trees by the school on 2nd, a shaded break away from the busy side of the street. It is a place for me to catch my breath, to hide in plain sight, to plan the rest of the route. I can see the corner of High Street. I can see which people to avoid, which way I should walk next.

Navigating the circular grates around the trees by 5th. I like the way they lean to one side, how the roots mythically rise from in between the crevices. I like the texture of the carved graffiti bark under my hands. They form a lost, forgotten ruin in plain sight.

Downtown, on the quiet strip under the neon lights of the Asian restaurant sign, shaded from sun where the cool breeze flows through, I watch the way the colors change on the sidewalk throughout the day, from muted sunrise to the glorious luminescence of nightfall.

Where the red bricks are missing on 15th and High, I know to go all the way to the road or watch carefully to avoid twisting an ankle. I look to see what treasures have fallen into them. I often watch from the crosswalk across the street to see people trip on the unfamiliar terrain. I can't help but smirk, knowing that I see what is unseen.

Where "Punx" is carved in a block of sidewalk that once signaled I was almost to my apartment, is now more a sign of what is absent than present.

Under the crumbling bits beneath the train bridge to Milo-Grogan, the graffiti is protected from weathering. The artists must have known that their work would be seen by pedestrians who move slow enough to read it, to stare, to interpret, to remember. This path usually leads me to the outskirts of town, a place where I can find some semblance of home. I'm heading there to glimpse it, to see if I can be *in* place again.

New sidewalks have been installed around the new factory, bright and hot next to the new pavement in the sun. The trees have been removed. I feel too exposed here. Everything has changed. Nothing has changed.

I move quickly to get to familiar ground, to a space that feels like a place, where I can look up and see what is around me, where I can exist with people that look and love like me. I arrive at last to the old school-turned-artist colony and its community garden. It is in places like this where I feel it the most, the lurking quiet that waits for a stranger to find it, hidden from view in a city of millions. The sounds of the street muffled, away from the cigarette smoke. The monarchs will be here soon; the bees have already arrived.

In the parking lot next to the garden, a stage has been erected for outdoor performances. Bands are playing, and someone has set up a small donation bucket on the merchandise table in the back. I am home, in a place that's never really felt like home, with my queer family, for just one night. This is the small sliver, the sacred space.

When darkness consumes I return to familiar sidewalks. I don't look down though. Best to let these ones go unnoticed for just one night. I let my attention go to the empty houses sleeping between full ones, to the empty streets, to the buzzing cicadas. The scale is still manageable here. There are still people within these buildings who, when without, show resistance, pride, and community. I wonder what will happen to this place with its already-too-bright-sidewalks? I hope it gets better. I hope nothing gets better.

Life in Franklinton

GREG PHILLIPS

Parts of the Franklinton neighborhood have become a developer's darling lately. New high-end apartments and condos are going up where blight once was. This scenario has played out in other neighborhoods bordering downtown Columbus, while near west side just sat idle in a slow downward spiral. It wasn't always like that. As the first urban settlement in what is now Columbus, Franklinton's development has been shaped by everything from the steam engine to the opioid epidemic. Somewhere in between all of that, two big floods did a one-two punch to seal the area's fate as a decaying neighborhood.

When I arrived in 1999, the neighborhood was still in a state of decay. Fresh out of college and into a new job, I had rented in and around downtown before. In the short list of areas close to downtown in my budget, Franklinton seemed to have the most potential. I thought it strange that so large a concentration of poor mostly white people could exist so close to a vibrant downtown. After all, I thought, how could such poverty exist this close to everything for too much longer?

Despite having Appalachian charm, Franklinton was rough socially and physically. The dense population of mostly poor people made the community a breeding ground for non-profits anxious to treat the surface effects of poverty—as long as the federal dollars were pouring in. This abuse led to local resentment for most kinds of authority, a true Appalachian trait. Despite that, there are good things about living here, like the close-knit culture of porch-based socialization.

As a native North Carolinian, I understood some aspects of backwoods culture, but Franklinton was unlike anything I had seen or experienced before. Living here has changed my ideas about the working and not-so-working poor.

The promise and potential of a new floodwall was still years away when I arrived, but its completion would lift many insurance regulations that limited new investment for decades. For that reason, my nearly 100-year-old house easily fit my budget and cost less than the average new Lexus. Despite my ideal location near a library and easy access to downtown and highways, my street had its share of problems. Bad social habits, criminal activity, and not enough people who cared still characterize the area.

I know I was not the first to move into the neighborhood expecting eventual change, but it felt like it. I remember taking up the sport of running and being the only person I saw jogging for miles in any direction. That sort of isolation was the norm back then.

Adjusting to Appalachian social norms was the toughest challenge. Neighbors were slow to warm up to me. It took nearly two years before that would happen. The turning point came when I stood up to two teenage boys who lived across the street. They constantly yelled various insults and names at me whenever they saw me outside. At first I just blew if off as something dumb kids did. I was never bullied as a teen, but this felt like high school. After yelling *nigger, spic,* or *faggot* from their bikes they'd just ride away. My house was nothing special, but it was well-kept, making my middle class values stick out as snooty to some. That may have been compounded by the fact that I was also the only brown person on my block.

The taunts would happen at random times, sometimes when I had company or when I was getting home from work.

One day while sitting on my porch with my laptop, the two boys rode up to their porch and started the insults when they saw me, like usual. They were just loud enough for me to hear, but always at a distance.

After thinking about it for a second, I put the computer down, got up, and walked over across the street to confront the boys. They seemed a bit shocked that I would. I said to them: "If you think I'm such a faggot or nigger why don't you just knock me da fuck out instead of yelling and running away like the trash you are?" My anger meant that I was able to channel my most authoritative Southern negro voice. They were not swayed.

Little did they know that I had just completed a non-credit self-defense course at The Ohio State University six months before. I never thought I would ever use any of it, but after experiencing a foiled mugging attempt in Olde Towne East, it seemed like a good idea. I was simply tired of the taunts. After addressing the surprised pair in front of the duplex, I turned around and walked back to my porch. To my surprise, they followed me. Just as I was about to turn around and sit, the older one hit me just above my right eye—surprising the hell out of me.

In my mind, all sorts of pent-up anger was released as the protective new homeowner in me thought, "Oh hell no, you did not just hit me on my property!"

At that point, long dormant impulses kicked in as I unloaded a quick punch across the kid's jaw (with the proper fighting stance of course). My instructor would have been proud. It happened so fast. The kid hit the ground while his friend ran away and got on his bike. Then it struck me that I just knocked out a teenager, as he scurried away like an injured dog. I just knew I would be in trouble with his parents or worse, the police. As I pondered that and began to worry, I could see neighbors standing outside, all looking (many clapping and laughing).

Later, various people who witnessed the incident congratulated me for standing up to them, and they all seemed to have wondered how long it would take before I would "take care of them." I never heard anything from either kids' parents. It's funny how it all played out. After that everyone spoke to me. Even the kids on the block would say, "Hi, Mr. Greg." People I didn't even know knew my name would speak to me. After that, everyone was fine with me, and eventually our preconceived notions about each other just sort of faded away as I became good friends with my neighbors.

Since that time the neighborhood has gone through many positive changes physically and socially. The pace of change has accelerated lately with new homes and residents spreading westward. The first noticeable wave came with the neo-hippie types obsessed with fresh vegetables. They came in with their utopian ideals from OSU and set up shop by applying their grassroots aesthetics to homes complete with gardens next door on what was once vacant land. They meant well with talk of food deserts and such, but were not always well received, maybe for some of the same reasons I had not been.

They set the stage for others to follow, like artists looking for cheap studio space. That's when the changes really started happening. Cities have always pimped artists for economic development of blighted areas, then abandoned them as market forces take over. It happened in the Short North. The jury is still out as to whether such a scenario will play out in Franklinton.

Once the terraforming started accelerating, the eastern edge of the neighborhood became hip and edgy, attracting hordes of young mostly white people with craft beer, single-speed bikes, and fancy beards. Some of those people settled into new or renovated homes in other parts of the neighborhood, encouraging some slum landlords to either patch up their properties or sell. This in turn has created a dynamic where it's possible to have beautiful new or renovated homes next to eyesores populated by some of the poorest people in Central Ohio.

People talk about gentrification and its negative effects, but the eastern parts of Franklinton have been immune so far. Eventually as more people consider the rest of the neighborhood, some renters (the dominant population) will be displaced because they simply cannot afford so-called workforce housing. Despite what the social and urban planners are saying, the dream of a mixed-income Franklinton is just not possible, especially when there are so many low-income people joining the ranks of the poor due to lack of education and certifiable skills.

I know the poor have to live somewhere. At the rate the neighborhood's changing, most of them won't be my neighbors for too long. Likely, sections of Franklinton will remain the same, but blight will not be as visually prominent as it is now. As a homeowner, I hope that the area can keep enough of its Appalachian charm while supporting true diversity. History tells me that's not likely to happen anytime soon.

Breakfast with Columbus

NICK DEKKER

The *New York Post* once called Columbus a "breakfast mecca." It's absolutely true. That means our city is a destination for the morning meal; people could and should travel here just to eat bacon and eggs and pancakes and donuts and coffee and eggs benedicts.

You'll get no argument from me. Columbus, where I've lived since 2002, has been a defining place for me on many levels: finishing grad school, getting our first "real life" jobs, buying a house, having kids, etc. It's been the place where it's all happened. Breakfast in Columbus has served as a home and guide to me over the years. Post graduate school, I was apparently looking for another writing project, so I started a little blog on a free Blogspot site and called it Breakfast With Nick. This was 2007, when Facebook was a baby, and Instagram and Twitter didn't exist. At that time, all of our friends and family kept personal blogs—that was how we kept up with each other over distance. My wife Beth and I had a little family blog that mostly featured pictures of the garden and the dog and eventually kids, so naturally, when I felt like recording the cool breakfast places we found in Columbus or as we traveled, I fired up a little blog and started writing. Eventually that turned into writing for other people about breakfast (and then other meals), and then into publishing my own guidebook to breakfast in Columbus, and then leading culinary tours, and on and on.

I've been asked "Why breakfast?" on many occasions. Why a blog about breakfast? Why is breakfast your thing? Are you weird or something? Aside from the obvious reply of "Why not breakfast?" my answer is that it's in my blood.

First off, I'm one of those insufferable morning people. When I have a day off, I look forward to getting up early. I love a quiet house, a cup of coffee, time to read or write. Sleeping in actually throws off my schedule. Ever since I was a kid, I always thrilled at the thought of going to breakfast the following day. I couldn't imagine more exciting words than "Let's go to breakfast tomorrow morning." I loved (and still love) making plans, going out in the morning, and starting the day with a meal in a crowded cafe or diner.

The morning always has so much potential. It's the start to a new day. All of your plans lay before you. And the morning meal boasts of all the possibilities. I especially love starting the day in the midst of a busy restaurant. Already you see people hard at work, fueling up for a busy day. People holding meetings. Friends reconnecting. Families enjoying a meal together. Going out to breakfast, you get to share in the start of everyone's day, not just your own.

Second, I was born, raised, and educated in Grand Rapids, Michigan, and GR is, amongst other things, an amazing breakfasting city. Grand Rapidians take their breakfast seriously, and eat it all the time. Business meeting? Go to Marie Catrib's. College class discussion? Meet up at Wolfgang's. Going out with the family on Saturday? Head to Real Food Cafe. Being from Grand Rapids is akin to putting "professional breakfaster" on your resume.

When I was younger, my paternal grandfather used to take one of his grandsons to breakfast every Saturday morning. He rotated each week between me and my brothers Mike and

Dan. He took us the same time, every Saturday, and always to the same place, although he gave us the illusion of choosing where to go. It was like the Model-T Ford: you could go anywhere you wanted for breakfast, as long as you wanted to go to Arnie's. (One week I even suggested a different restaurant. Grandpa willingly took me there, sipping on coffee while I ate eggs and toast. When I was finished, he said, "Are you done? Good, let's go to Arnie's.") Arnie's was a comfortable and welcoming place, but I think one of the real reasons he took us there was because he knew *everybody* there. We'd stroll by the booths and hear everyone say, "Hi, Marty!" He'd make chit-chat and introduce his grandson. It was like he owned the place. When he passed away unexpectedly in 1987, my grandmother found, penciled in his day planner, the next couple weeks' worth of breakfasts. Each Saturday was labeled with one of our names: Mike, then Nick, then Dan.

But while I learned to love breakfast in Grand Rapids, Columbus breakfast is where I flourished. In a funny way, the breakfast scene in Columbus has helped define who I am. It's allowed me to meet a slew of incredible, hardworking people. It's taught me to love and explore my city, to venture out and get to know it in ways I normally wouldn't. It's taught me the value of community, of supporting the people and businesses around you. Most of all, it's shown me how food, while a basic necessity, is an important place where people can gather and connect.

So what qualifies Columbus as a "breakfast mecca"?

Columbus is many things. Ohio's capital city. The largest city in the state. The fourteenth largest in the country. Home to a gigantic research one university, with high-profile athletic programs. Located in the middle of farmland. Full of revitalized historic districts, sprawling suburbs, and a re-awakening downtown. With a bustling arts scene, a healthy appetite for sports, and several financial centers. Traditional and progressive. A landlocked Midwestern city named for a fifteenth-century Italian explorer.

Breakfast in Columbus is many things as well. It's a perfect crossroads between the traditional and the innovative. You'll find a good dose of history and a healthy sense of exploration.

We enjoy a healthy diner culture. Every neighborhood, every suburb has a diner to call its own. German Village Coffee Shop in German Village, Creekside Cafe in Gahanna, Beechwold Diner in Beechwold, Jack & Benny's near campus, Dan's Drive-In on the south side. Diners are not fancy or sophisticated; the food doesn't vary much between them, but they're community hubs. Regulars gather to exchange news. Owners and servers know people's orders. Multiple generations sit in the same booths and at the same stools at the same counters. The atmosphere is light-hearted and convivial, and smells strongly of bacon. Although there are some newer kids on the block in Columbus, we feature plenty of institutions that date back to the 40s, 50s, and 60s: Jack's Diner downtown started in 1942, Chef-O-Nette in Upper Arlington has been around since the early 50s, Nancy's first started in 1968.

Nancy's trajectory highlights the importance of diners in Columbus breakfast culture. A woman named Nancy started it in 1968, quickly grew tired of it, and sold it to Cindy King a year later. Cindy ran it until she was forced to retire for health reasons in 2009. The diner was in need of serious upgrades, and she made the decision to close. But Clintonville would not let it go quietly. Contractors who dined there donated their time to repair the floors, the equipment, the ceiling, the HVAC. The nearby Lowe's donated materials. Generations of regulars, who felt indebted to Cindy because of her hospitality, sent in checks to pay her back. Barely nine months after closing, Cindy's niece Sheila re-opened the diner, and Clintonville once again filled the tiny booths and the stools around the U-shaped counters. When Sheila herself passed away a couple years later, her husband Rick kept the doors open, and it's been going strong ever since. As a general rule, you never say anything bad about someone's neighborhood diner. It gets personal very quickly, and the story of Nancy's demonstrates that.

But Columbus breakfast is defined by more than diners. The brunch craze has fully suffused Columbus dining culture, so that every hip restaurant in the Short North, plenty of food trucks and breweries, every swanky dining spot across the city offers some form of brunch. I usually joke on my Columbus Food Adventures brunch tour that brunch is a brilliant business model: you take your popular dishes, add eggs to them, and no one judges you for serving alcohol at 10 a.m.

While Columbus is good with old school diners, I think it's a balance of interesting and innovative restaurants that puts us in destination territory. Think pancake balls and sweet and spicy bacon at Katalina's. Or those beautiful, flaky croissants at Pistacia Vera. Or the breakfast roll on house-made brioche at Cravings Cafe. Or the akoori, spicy Indian scrambled eggs, at The Table. Or that unfairly good egg sandwich at Fox in the Snow. Or those colorful chilaquiles at Starliner Diner. Or the Czech-by-way-of-Texas kolaches stuffed with eggs, cheese, chorizo, and jalapenos at Kolache Republic. Or the breakfast burrito at Northstar Cafe. Or the ube waffles with chicken at Bonifacio. Or the fried egg tacos at Explorers Club.

I think you can see where I'm going. Columbus blends new and old very well. Traditional and creative. From corned beef hash at a diner to pork sausages with rice at a Filipino eatery.

And I haven't even touched on donuts and coffee.

Breakfast is the pulse of a city. If you want to get to know a new place, go find a local breakfast spot. Whenever we visit a new city, we seek out five benchmarks: a breakfast joint, a brewery, a coffee shop, donuts, and a park (to walk off the breakfast, beer, and donuts). At those five places you'll find the locals, you'll get to interact with them, and you'll get a sense of what that community is truly about.

That's Columbus. If you want to get to know us, have breakfast with us.

Consider the Johnny Marzetti

SHELLEY MANN HITE

Columbus isn't synonymous with one particular dish the way Cincinnati is with chili, or Chicago is with deep-dish, or Philly is with cheesesteaks.

As Ohio's capital city and rapidly growing metropolis, this is disappointing. But it's not really surprising when you consider our city's well-known struggle to understand and articulate our own national brand. When you spend as much time as we do hemming and hawing over reputation, over what sets us apart, over what makes us special—in other words, over what everyone else thinks of us—it doesn't leave much time or energy for perfecting and promoting our own signature foodstuffs.

It's also important to remember that Columbus is in the midst of a massive population influx, with figures expected to swell to up to 3 million people by 2050. What if that means we don't know the story of our city yet? And if you don't know the story of your city, you can't know the story of your food. Indeed, it's likely that we don't have a signature food yet because up until now we've been preoccupied with trying to show the rest of the world that, while we may be smack in the middle of flyover country, we can still pull off impressive

French cuisine or Spanish tapas or a high-end seafood concept. In the last few years, though, I've started to see signs of the city's newest crop of chefs beginning to tell our own food story, and that's something that excites me greatly.

So what is an iconic local dish, anyway? I believe it's a food you can find only in a certain place, one that people will demand "you must try" while visiting that place, and one that you develop crazy cravings for upon moving away from that place. It's also not a dish you can find at only one restaurant—it's a concept that's always evolving because it inspires up-and-coming chefs to try their hand at improving upon it. You'll see locals fight over which restaurant makes it best. And the best of these dishes become so intertwined with that place that they take on the place's name—New York pizza, Philly Cheesesteak, North Carolina barbecue.

I grew up in Cincinnati, and we have no shortage of iconic local dishes there. Cincinnati chili is, of course, our pride and joy and the region's best-known dish. Cincinnatians argue over which local chain does it best, Skyline or Gold Star, and whether either of those can hold a candle to the versions found at independent chili parlors like Camp Washington Chili. The allure of the Cincinnati 3-way (spaghetti topped with chili and shredded cheddar) can be in big part attributed to that magical layer where the heat from the cinnamon-spiked chili sauce has melted the base of the mountain of cheese. If you're from Cincinnati, too, you'll know exactly what I mean. Then you have things like goetta, a spiced mush made with sausage and pinhead oats that's found primarily in the Cincinnati area and is celebrated each year at Goettafest on the downtown riverfront.

In 2014 the *Columbus Dispatch*'s new food editor, a recent transplant from the Akron area, was perplexed by our city's lack of a recognized official food. So the *Dispatch* asked readers to crown Columbus's official food, and a resounding majority chose Schmidt's Bahama Mama. Runners-up included the White Castle Slider, the Schmidt's cream puff, the buckeye candy, and Columbus-style pizza.

Served at Schmidt's Sausage Haus und Restaurant in German Village, the Bahama Mama is spicy German-style beef and pork sausage smoked over hickory, packing some heat with Schmidt's secret spice blend. It can be ordered over hot kraut as part of a sausage platter, but it's best enjoyed on a toasted buttery split-top bun with sauerkraut and spicy mustard.

The Bahama Mama offers a nice nod to our city's significant German heritage. Germans were among the earliest white settlers of Ohio, and numerous German communities popped up across the state. The Schmidt family, owners of Schmidt's Sausage Haus and creators of the Bahama Mama, joined an influx of German immigrants in a working-class neighborhood on the south side of Columbus that would become known as German Village. The Schmidts began making the German sausages in the 1880s out of the J. Fred Schmidt Meat Packing House in the neighborhood, which evolved to resemble a mini version of Germany. Over the decades, German Village has become the city's pride and joy success story: a genuine preserved historic district that doubles as our most charming neighborhood, home to a number of restaurants, bars, galleries, and boutiques.

The Schmidt's Bahama Mama does pass the "you must try" test. But isn't everyone really saying, "You must visit German Village!"? While there are plenty better restaurants in the Village (Pistacia Vera! Skillet! G. Michael's! Lindey's!) there's no more German Village-y restaurant than Schmidt's. The longtime establishment has all the characteristics of a tourist trap, from ye olde German font to the costumed waitstaff to the perpetual long lines to the food that always somehow tastes better in your memories of it. More troublesome, Columbus certainly isn't the only place you can find authentic German-style sausages.

So can we admit that what we really love so much about the Bahama Mama is the funny name? It's fitting, given our city's infamous inferiority complex, that our official food's name brings to mind a tropical paradise offering an escape from Columbus. The story goes that the sausage's "spicy-hot" factor reminded one Schmidt's family member of a particularly memorable 1960s trip to the Bahamas. This "wild" uncle purportedly proposed the name to commemorate a dalliance with a local woman (and not after an evening spent downing the eponymous rum drinks).

Honestly, all power to the *Dispatch* for attempting to nail down our city's official food. It's no easy feat. There's a distinct lack of dishes we can claim were actually "invented" here in Columbus. Well, except for Johnny Marzetti.

As legend has it, this ground beef casserole dish was indeed invented in Columbus, and it's by far our most widely known dish. (A variant called "Johnny Mazetti" has become a beloved dish in Panama.) But for some inexplicable reason, we—and I include myself here—have a hard time accepting Johnny Marzetti as our signature dish.

Bizarrely, T. Marzetti Company, the company widely acknowledged as introducing the dish, outright refuses to take the credit. According to the Ohio History Connection, the story goes that Ohioan Teresa Marzetti, an Italian immigrant, was the first person to serve the casserole Johnny Marzetti in a restaurant: Marzetti's, opened in 1896 at 10th Avenue and North High Street near The Ohio State University. Priced at 45 cents, the dish became popular with Ohio State students before catching the attention of Columbus Public Schools. Johnny Marzetti quickly became a staple on school cafeteria menus throughout the state, then a favorite of budget-conscious home cooks after the recipe was published in a number of mid-century magazines and cookbooks.

But T. Marzetti Company spokespeople say there's no concrete evidence—presumably in the form of a printed menu or a recipe card—to prove the dish originated at the restaurant.

And you'll be hard-pressed to find the dish on any restaurant menus around the city. *Columbus Monthly*'s Eric Lyttle explored the dish's downfall in a story in January 2018 titled "The Disappearance of Johnny Marzetti."

One notable exception is at Service Bar, the highly lauded restaurant offering at Middle West Spirits distillery in the Short

North, where Chef Avishar Barua has offered his own twists on the dish. Barua grew up here in Columbus in a Bangladeshi household, and has said he always loved eating Johnny Marzetti in the school cafeteria growing up. The dish is not one of Service Bar's most Instagrammed, but its inclusion was plenty intriguing to the local food writers who covered the opening. All of them mentioned Marzetti on the menu in early features. When I spotted that dish on his menu, I had to smile. I have, I can admit, played my own role in downplaying the influence of Johnny Marzetti. Several years ago, I had proposed what I thought to be an ingenious idea. I put out a challenge to local chefs to invent a new signature Columbus dish to be unveiled at Independents' Day, our annual music, beer, and food festival celebrating all things independent and local. I envisioned a half-dozen dishes served from a tent throughout the fest, with festival-goers sampling the offerings and voting on the favorite. At the end of the weekend, we'd crown a new Columbus icon—and we'd all come together behind the thing, slap Columbus's name on it, and get to work promoting the hell out of it.

As a quick side note, this thought has crossed my mind: what if the name Columbus is our problem? There are 18 cities named Columbus in the U.S. We still have to specify ours by attaching *Ohio* to it, for crying out loud. Add that to the fact that we're named after a certain explorer/pillager that many would prefer not to continue to celebrate, and it's clear that Columbus brings with it some baggage. This, of course, becomes problematic not just in terms of naming our iconic food but also in establishing our very identity as a city.

One way to fix both problems would be to change Columbus's name, a drastic publicity stunt that I've long been rooting for. Granted, I'm an admitted let's-just-burn-it-all-down type and odds are this will never, ever happen. But consider, for a moment, just how much easier this branding exercise would be if we lived in a place called Ohio City? Right?

Anyhow, the inspiration to invent Columbus's signature dish harkened back to the old World's Fair days, when countries would come together to show off state-of-the-art science and technology achievements as well as new foodstuffs. Take, for example, the 1904 World's Fair held in St. Louis, Missouri, where the following all-star list of foods purportedly made their debut: the hamburger, the hot dog, peanut butter, iced tea, the club sandwich, cotton candy, and the ice cream cone. While a careful examination of history will show that many, if not most, of those food items existed before the World's Fair, this particular international gathering happened to take place at a time when the American foodways were rapidly expanding, and shined a bright spotlight on the new modern American cuisine. It introduced new foods like French's yellow mustard and Dr. Pepper to a mass audience, which in turn began to spread the gospel of American fast food.

What if something similar is going on here in Columbus? What if the reason we don't have an iconic dish is because we haven't yet forged our own Columbus foodways? What if our current proliferation of talented chefs is rewriting our city's food story into something new that we can't quite see yet because we're right in the middle? What if something much bigger is on the horizon?

At the time I had this idea, Chef Barua happened to be on a culinary hiatus of sorts. He'd been hired by Middle West Spirits to helm their new restaurant, but with the restaurant opening still quite a ways off he was spending his days researching food via trips abroad and test kitchen experimentation. I asked him to help in recruiting chefs who might be up for the challenge of inventing Columbus's signature dish.

Chef Barua's curiosity was piqued. But after chatting with colleagues across the city, he wasn't able to find anyone with the, let's say, *chutzpah* to single-handedly invent an iconic Columbus dish. Instead, he proposed, what if we brought together a group of chefs who would offer their own take on what we can all safely agree is a famous dish that originated in Columbus: the Johnny Marzetti?

Yup. The Johnny Marzetti. My soul sank. Are we doomed to be the town that invented a dish hyped as "simple, easy, and cheap to make"? A homestyle Hamburger Helper? I was skeptical we could attract crowds of people interested in sampling Marzetti variations, so the Marzetti throwdown never came to pass.

Why do we hate the Johnny Marzetti? What is it that disappoints us? In an attempt to understand why we collectively cringe at the idea of Marzetti as our essential dish, I embarked on a quest to untangle my own troubled relationship to the dish.

Not helping matters is my longtime aversion to ground beef (my signature chili is made with chopped sirloin, and I'm far more likely to make a tuna noodle casserole than anything starring ground chuck). Aesthetics and taste aside, though, it's the dish's immediate cultural associations that turn me off. For starters, it's inextricably linked to school cafeterias—one step above prison food on the appetizing cuisine scale.

Beyond that, Marzetti taps into Buckeye fever, one of my least favorite aspects of living in Columbus. The dish's origin story centers on Ohio State, my alma mater. I enjoyed my time there, but I'm most certainly not a rabid Buckeye fan, and I wince whenever someone mischaracterizes Columbus as a glorified college town.

Finally, Johnny Marzetti just feels . . . boring. And isn't that what the chip on our collective shoulder is all about? If this is the dish that represents Columbus, then does that mean we're really as bland as they all think we are? A desperation casserole designed to feed the masses for cheap? Can't we do better than that?

In my quest to find a way to start to love the Marzetti, I started by seeking the dish out at restaurants around town. I've spotted it as an occasional daily special at Tee Jaye's Country Place and a few other similar down-home diners. But one reliable spot to find Johnny Marzetti is Weiland's Market, an independent, family-owned grocery less than a block south of the T. Marzetti Company headquarters in Clintonville. Weiland's version is made with a mozzarella-provolone blend and a heavy blanket of shredded parmesan over a macaroni and ground beef casserole with green peppers and mushrooms. You'll always find it in the prepared foods case, and it's an ideal introductory Marzetti course.

Next I headed to Service Bar to try Chef Barua's twist on the dish. His original version, the Michelone Marzetti, got its moniker from the distillery's Oyo Michelone Reserve Bourbon, and offered a rustic take on the classic with hand-made creste di gallo ("rooster's crest") pasta in a 12-hour tomato sauce served with an oversized meatball and two slabs of garlic bread.

Barua improved upon his own recipe for an updated version, the audacious Hearth Baked Marzetti. Order it and you got a cast-iron skillet loaded with that same creste di gallo pasta in a lovely Ragu alla Bolognese inspired by Middle West Spirits owner Ryan Lang's family recipe, topped with a layer of mozzarella. *And then* it was covered in a thick layer of garlic bread dough and baked until golden in a wood stone oven. It's a play on pot pie, but with a starch-on-starch combo that's essentially unheard of in today's carb-conscious society. This was aggressive comfort fare. I made it through a third of the skillet, and wasn't hungry until dinner the next day. I adored it.

My restaurant taste tests complete, I set about making the "mother recipe" in my home kitchen. While the Johnny Marzetti has been endlessly customized and reinterpreted by home cooks, the Original Johnny Marzetti recipe as memorialized in the Ohio History Center is as follows:

3 tablespoons olive oil
1 large onion, chopped
¾ pound mushrooms, cleaned and sliced
2 pounds lean ground beef
3 ½ cups tomato sauce
1 ½ pounds cheddar cheese, shredded
1 pound elbow macaroni, cooked and drained.

Saute onion in oil until limp, about 3 minutes. Add mushrooms and fry until juices are released, about 5 minutes. Add beef and cook, stirring, breaking into clumps, until no longer red. Remove from heat and mix in tomato sauce and all but 1 cup of cheese. Transfer to greased 9-by-13 baking dish and add macaroni. Toss gently to mix. Scatter remaining cheese on top. Bake, uncovered, in 350-degree oven until browned and bubbling, about 35 to 40 minutes.

I found the casserole immensely satisfying. The shockingly large amount of shredded cheddar makes for a molten cheese sauce that's simultaneously smile-inducing and soul-warming. My Marzetti slab left behind a pool of orangey-red grease that I fondly remember from elementary lunch trays.

Here's the weird part: This Marzetti didn't taste like what I thought I remembered eating growing up. If we're being honest, I was always more of a packed-lunch than a cafeteria-lunch person, and my mom never cooked Marzetti for my brothers and me. In fact, she wasn't an illustrious home cook by any stretch of the imagination. But she did make a similar casserole with Italian sausage, rotini, and mozzarella. In general her casseroles rank among my fondest childhood food memories. Chicken and rice casserole, "orange noodle" casserole made with tomato sauce and sour cream, egg and sausage breakfast casserole every Christmas morning.

In short, this casserole tasted like home.

I thought, then, about moving away from Ohio and moving back home—such a common story among those of us who live in Columbus.

My heart belongs to Ohio. And the thing about that is I never wanted it to. I grew up in Ohio and wanted to get out of here as fast as I could. I hightailed it to Atlanta the second I graduated college. But whenever I came back to visit, I can't explain it—I felt like my circadian rhythms were realigning. And when I moved back in 2007, I felt everything shift back into focus.

As much as I didn't want to be in Ohio, I could tell deep inside that I belonged here.

In the South, things were different in big ways but also down to the smallest details. Tall, skinny Eastern white pines replaced the grand oak and elm trees I grew up with, screeching katydids and cicadas dominated the night sounds rather than the calming crickets I was used to, and instead of soil the ground was made of hard red clay.

The warm seasons started earlier, and lasted longer. At first that seemed like a gift, but what I came to understand was spring doesn't seem as sweet when you haven't all just barely made it through winter alive.

Winter is exactly when Marzetti becomes a necessary addition to the Midwestern meal rotation. Just as you'll see across the rest of the region, we Columbusites love our casseroles. When I asked friends for their Marzetti memories, most immediately recognized the dish under some other name. One friend said her mom always made a hamburger casserole with rotini—"We called it Boingy Noodles."

Search for Johnny Marzetti on Pinterest, and you'll discover a number of similar casseroles will appropriate the name Marzetti even though they're more technically an American Goulash (simply ground beef and elbow macaroni in tomato sauce) or American Chop Suey (all of the above plus onions and mushrooms). What sets Marzetti apart from those lesser casseroles is that molten cheese factor.

What I realized is my knee-jerk anti-Marzetti reaction could partially be explained by the fact that all along I'd been misremembering the dish as one of those other joyless, cheeseless versions. I'd been imagining a fairly dry, pasta-heavy casserole with a sprinkling of shredded cheese on top.

Armed with a better understanding of what makes Marzetti special, I challenged myself: Could I make some updates to the mother recipe and find an easy home kitchen version I'd be proud to tout as Columbus's own?

I spent some time pondering the crucial components that made a casserole a Johnny Marzetti. Marzetti, I decided, should be cheap, filling, and easily made with ingredients you probably already have in your fridge and pantry. The four key ingredients are pasta, meat, tomato sauce and cheese.

For my second iteration, I swapped out macaroni for the wide egg noodles common in Ohio's Amish country. I went with ground pork rather than beef, and increased the vegetable level by adding in some red bell pepper, chopped fresh tomatoes and fresh basil and rosemary to accompany the traditional mushrooms and onions. I kept the sharp cheddar. When making the Marzetti sauce, it's crucial to continue adding in cheese way past the point where it seems like you've added plenty. It should feel kind of like you're making a queso dip.

Johnny Marzetti 2.0 was a tasty variation. My husband said we should call it "Ohio's lasagna," a moniker inspired by the wide, flat egg noodles and also because I left it in the oven a few minutes too long while putting the baby to bed. The rubberized cheese topping did bear a distinct resemblance to Stouffer's frozen lasagna. Those extra vegetables lightened the dish a bit, and the fresh herbs mixed into a simple heirloom tomato sauce made for a fresh, bright flavor profile. I definitely preferred the juicer ground pork to standard ground beef.

But this still felt like a fairly traditional ground-something-or-other casserole. For my second variation, I wanted to try something less expected. I liked the idea of incorporating a more luxurious meat component, like tender braised beef short ribs. But I didn't want to abandon the idea of this being a quick and easy dinner recipe, so braising the ribs in a Dutch oven for hours was not really a viable option. Instead, I turned to a thoroughly modern, super trendy solution: my Instant Pot.

First I seared bone-in beef short ribs on saute mode until they were nicely browned on all sides. I pulled the ribs and set them aside while sautéing onions, red bell peppers and sliced mushrooms until tender. Then the short ribs went back into the Instant Pot, along with tomato sauce, herbs, and a cup of red wine. While the meat sauce pressure-cooked for 35 minutes, I boiled my pasta—a heartier cavatappi inspired by Service Bar's robust creste di gallo rooster's crests. I'd loved how toothsome that pasta was, a welcome contrast to the mushy over-boiled macaroni noodles found in the cafeteria versions.

Once the meat sauce depressurized, I fished out the short ribs and shredded the perfectly cooked meat, cranked the Instant Pot back up to sauté to reduce the sauce, then stirred in lots and lots of cheddar—the one ingredient I just couldn't let go. When it was time to combine the pasta and the sauce in the casserole dish, I upped the ratio of meat sauce and cut back on the noodles—but kept the cheese the same. The whole concoction went into a casserole dish topped with hefty handfuls of cheese before baking at 350 for 35 minutes.

Marzetti 3.0 was very good, and I'd consider busting it out for a fancier dinner party. The short ribs definitely elevate the Marzetti, making it feel more like an indulgence than a budget-stretcher. And I prefer this saucier casserole made with a heartier pasta to the lightly sauced elbow-mac recipes.

But, in all honesty, after all that hand-wringing I preferred the mother recipe best.

At the end of my kitchen experimentation, I thought back to Chef Avishar Barua at Service Bar and his decision to include Johnny Marzetti on his first few menus. His menu tells a story of food in Columbus through the lens of his own personal relationship with the city. Just like me, and so many of us, he left Columbus for a few years (to cook at acclaimed restaurants like New York's Mission Chinese and WD-50) before returning home. In continuing to revisit the dish over the years, his message is this: We already have our signature dish. It's time to stop looking.

So how do we go about coalescing around Johnny Marzetti as our signature dish?

For starters, it'd be great if we could get T. Marzetti Co. on board. OK, so Johnny Marzetti was never on the menus in the restaurants. What if it was a chalkboard special? What if it was a secret, off-menu item? The legend has been repeated so many times by this point, it seems comical to go to such efforts to refute it.

Food origin stories are notoriously murky. Do you know how many people claim to have invented the ice cream cone? We all love a good story—and it doesn't have to be 100% verifiable to satisfy our curiosity. Does it really matter where exactly in Columbus the dish originated? Even if we can't agree that Johnny Marzetti was invented at Marzetti's, it's hard to argue with the fact that the dish first gained national traction because it was served in Columbus Public Schools cafeterias and, later, school lunchrooms across the Midwest.

Columbus should be capitalizing on Johnny Marzetti as our iconic dish. T. Marzetti should be selling jars of "Johnny Marzetti Sauce" next to the marinara on grocery shelves across the country. More of our chefs should be taking inspiration from this humble pasta dish. And we all need to start saying, "You must try the Johnny Marzetti!"

Accepting Johnny Marzetti is about embracing what we already have instead of waiting breathlessly for the new next thing. It's about making peace with the essence of our city *as it has been known up until now* and not worrying about what is to come.

In the end, yes, Johnny Marzetti is food for the masses. And isn't that exactly what we need in Columbus at this particular moment?

Flat City Nights

ROBERT LOSS

What Ain't to Be, Just Might Happen

The second side of *The Gibson Brothers Build a Raft*, a 1986 cassette release, starts with the band being introduced at Avondale Elementary School by one Essie Richardson, a teacher or maybe the principal. We're in the Columbus neighborhood of Franklinton, just west of downtown where the Scioto River and Olentangy River meet. Presumably the Gibson Brothers—who are not brothers—wait behind Richardson as she explains in her over-enunciated teacher-voice, "We've certainly run the gamut this year in terms of looking at different cultural activities. We've been to the ballet, we've been to the symphony, and now we're going to do something entirely different." As an electric guitar yawns awake, you can hear the clenched enthusiasm in Richardson's voice when she adds: "Rock and roll!" One child shouts "Yay!" Feedback burps behind her. Richardson backtracks: "But not so much rock and roll as you know it today." Feedback squeals. "Uh, they're going to do a little bit of country music."

The band peels off into the rollicking "Woo Hoo." Lead singer and guitarist "Country" Jeff Evans sings variations on the titular phrase and throws in a "Yeah!" "Rock!" and "That's right!" now and then. The children respond with tepid applause. Despite Richardson's introduction, it seems like the band has stolen into the school somehow. They slide into a punked-up version of "Hot Dog," a song recorded by Buck Owens under the pseudonym Corky Jones, then swagger through an almost unrecognizable "My Bucket's Got a Hole in It" and the Hank Mills tune "Walking Bum" before demolishing "Rubber Room," a song by Porter Wagoner first released on his 1972 psycho-country album *What Ain't to Be, Just Might Happen.*

There's nothing fancy or overtly educational about any of this. The recordings sound like bootlegs, like you just happen to be overhearing an ordinary event from eons ago. Through-out all of it, the Gibson Brothers sound entirely sincere and also like they can't give a damn. Rhythm guitarists Don How-land and Dan Dow split ears. (There's no bass, no bassist.) Drummer Ellen Hoover holds it together on a snare drum and floor tom.

Things get weird on "Mississippi Bo Weevil/Poem," a jaunty blues number. About two minutes in, Evans stops the band mid-stroll. "You know, my old man was a bread-stasher all his life," he drawls. "He never got fat and wound up with a used car, a seventeen-inch screen and *arthur-itis.* Tomorrow is a drag, man. Tomorrow is a king-sized bust." The band saun-ters back into the song but only for a bit. Another stop, an-other speech from Evans. Music. Speech. The kids are getting worked up, talking over the music and shouting back at the Brothers. More music. "Tomorrow is Dragsville, cats," Evans finally says. "Tomorrow is a *king-sized, motherfucking drag.*" The room erupts with delighted shrieks.

In the photograph of the band onstage at Avondale Ele-mentary, which graces the cover of *The Gibson Brothers Build a Raft,* Ellen Hoover is wearing a bolo tie, and she looks sympa-thetic to what's being inflicted upon the children of Avondale Elementary. For some of them, though, I suspect it was, to that point, the greatest day of their lives. . . .

Except that "Mississippi Bo Weevil/Poem" and most of the live recordings that precede it weren't recorded at Avondale

Elementary. They were recorded at various Columbus dive bars and clubs on the High Street strip running parallel to the Ohio State campus, including Bernie's and the Greek restaurant/rock bar Apollo's. Only "Woo Hoo," I think, comes from the school.

Listening to the album, nothing indicates this fact except that the kids at Avondale seem to be getting older as the set progresses, or else someone let in a pack of teenagers. There's no explanation in the liner notes, either. Nothing obvious prevents "Mississippi Bo Weevil/Poem" from having been recorded in front of an audience of Jams-wearing children sitting cross-legged on the floor of the school's gymnasium—nothing except common sense. Certainly no band would take advantage of their invitation to play country music for children by blasting through "Rubber Room" or by advising nine year-olds that "tomorrow is a king-sized motherfucking drag," right? Listening to . . . Build a Raft for the first time, I couldn't rule it out. And maybe because it defied common sense, I was convinced that it had happened. I liked the idea that Evans believed he had a message for those kids that day, that he was hell-bent on confronting those kids with his hick-punk philosophy, and that maybe he got a little carried away but, you know, it was all from the heart.

"That would have been a weird school," Howland would later tell me. "Those kids were, like, six years old. First and second grade. That would've been horribly wrong."

Pre-Fab City

I've been trying to figure out why the schism between authenticity and imagination, between the literal truth and the artistic truth presented on The Gibson Brothers Build a Raft stands in for what I think of the Columbus music "scene." Some of it must be the energy in the Gibson Brothers' hillbilly-meets-punk music, a genre our city is known for. Some of it is a loving appreciation for the sheer ridiculousness and carelessness of it all. (Howland again: "We weren't trying to trick anybody. I think we were probably just too lazy to write down where the stuff came from.") But in the final analysis, it's the allure of Columbus as an undefined place, an open set of variables, a flat landscape at a major American crossroads where anything can happen, where all rules can be subverted, and whatever someone from beyond I-270 considers to be authentic about Columbus can be turned on its head.

Here, authenticity is not something you're born with. You make your own.

That sounds grand and idealistic, I know, but over and over again it's what I hear in the music from this city. Instead of living up to the dictates of being from Cowtown, the home of a massive state university, Ohio's capitol, or any other preconceived notions about being a large Midwestern city, the music made in Columbus usually seems to have charted its own unique course by drawing from the wells of whatever's nearby, whatever's handy, whatever's desired.

Maybe that's because, for a time, the city has lacked its own character. Not long before I moved to Columbus in 2002, a musician friend described it as a "pre-fab city." The description seemed true. Every time I drove down from Cleveland to visit, a new building was popping up somewhere and chances were that it looked nondescript. The recently erected Arena District was indistinguishable from a hundred other cities' similar districts. Then there was the enormous shopping center Easton, a fake town designed to look quaint and suburban. Soon the southern portion of those High Street dive bars and clubs bordering Ohio State where the Gibson Brothers once played, along with the head shops and record stores and funky bagel restaurants, would be demolished for generic chain restaurants and sports bars. If the city had a history, you couldn't sense it.

For all of the consequences this campaign of bland had for the city's actual history and its overlooked citizens, it also meant there was no pattern, no set of rules, no singular tradition. That's how I've seen it, anyway, and that's why I've stayed: the open space, the freedom to do whatever. Without money you can't have much effect on the city's brick-and-mortar architecture, but within its cultural architecture you can fabricate something unique, you can try and fail and try again, and you can write history with and for the community rather than live up to someone's pre-fab idea of what an "authentic" Columbus should be.

One History of Columbus Music

The danger in this "anything goes" pseudo-utopian outlook is not just that it might ignore the barriers faced by people who are marginalized in art as they are in life. It's also that a blinding focus on the present and future might overlook the past and the accomplishments, stories, and art of those who lived in Columbus long before it started popping up on national "Best Cities" lists. I mean, it's not like Columbus doesn't have a musical history. Cultural authenticity often depends on history to define whatever an authentic "X" may be—"authentic" rap, "authentic" country music—and so maybe the fact that Columbus's musical history can't be captured by a simple image or a certain "sound" explains why, today, it seems like Columbus music can be anything it wants to be.

In its earliest days, Columbus music was the product of exoduses mainly from the South. Bronzeville bloomed during the Great Migration in the early twentieth century and became a thriving African-American neighborhood just east of downtown that was once described as a rival to Harlem. Now called King-Lincoln-Bronzeville, it was home to many doo-wop groups, like the 4 Pharaohs, formed in 1956, and best known for "Give Me Your Love," a song of pure desire. A decade and a half later, soul act the Four Mints were recording for the local label Capsoul. Their single "Row My Boat" begins with a piano trickle and glockenspiel drops—it's almost silly, but then there's a sudden rush outward, as if someone has opened the door of a claustrophobic apartment onto a blissful summer day.

Working-class blacks and whites traveled the road north that Dwight Yoakam, who was raised in Columbus, paid homage to in his song "Readin', Rightin', Route 23." Here in the city, Route 23 is High Street, Third and Fourth Street, Indianola Avenue, and then High Street again, but for thousands of families looking for jobs and carrying their culture with them, it was the highway out of the Jim Crow South, the tumult of the Civil Rights era, and the hills and coal mines of Kentucky and West Virginia alike. While many headed to points north like Toledo and Detroit, clearly a bunch of folks stayed in Columbus. If you can hear the story of black working-class innovators in groups like the Four Mints, and the story of white working-class migrants in Yoakam's neo-traditional honky-tonk music of the 1980s, it's true that those narratives became fainter as time passed. That's another reason why *The Gibson Brothers Build a Raft* stands out, I think: its fusion of country blues, rock, and punk holds America's musical history in its teeth.

Punk was the great break from tradition in American popular music, not so much in sound but in attitude and method. By attitude I mean "burn it down and start again," "No Future," and a total negation of societal values. Ironically, this is where you start to see some longevity, some influence coming out of Columbus, where the punk bands, as was the case everywhere else, had names like knives: the Twisted Shouts, the True Believers, Screaming Urge, Vertical Slit, the Blunt Stitches, the Naked Skinnies, La-Z Boys, the Vorpal Blades. There's a case to be made that Mike Rep and the Quotas' "Rocket to Nowhere," recorded in 1976 and released in 1978 on the California label Moxie, was the first punk recording in town. In time Mike "Rep" Hummel would be known almost as much for his production work as his own music. (Listen, for instance, to the Columbus shitgaze band Times New Viking's debut album, *Dig Yourself*. Rep once corrected me when I called it "lo-fi" music. "It's mega-fi," he said, meaning that it lets in *all* the noise.) Rep's career speaks to the way punk music changed the method of music production and distribution, otherwise known as the DIY aesthetic and ethic. In 1980, Tim Anstaett, a concert promoter, founded the zine *The Offense*. Half the writers were local musicians. Rep started the countertop label New Age that same year (and later changed its name to Old Age/ No Age). Along with Rep, Jim Shepard pioneered do-it-yourself recording here for his band Vertical Slit in the 1970s and Phantom Limb and Skullbank, along with his solo projects, into the 1980s.

Which brings us back, once again, to *The Gibson Brothers Build a Raft*. Mike Rep was the one who released it on cassette in 1986, and the one who, by all accounts, let a sucker like me think half of it featured the band playing for a gym full of increasingly rabid children.

None of the people I've mentioned had any authenticity to lean on other than the imagination and integrity they brought to the mic. Authenticity has a way of providing instant legitimacy by way of established narratives and familiar ideas about who can play what music, and with those, at least a certain amount of understandability and cachet. Columbus provided none of that. That's why this music, even when you hear it today, has so much power. It sounds like the musicians are making something from just about nothing.

Neither were they too concerned about creating a particular style or sound. I asked Tim Anstaett once if he thought *The Offense* conjured up a coherent portrait of the Columbus scene. "I'm sure that to a reader who had no other source of information about the town, all of the submissions might conjure up some sort of image," he said, "but I think it could only vaguely be described as involving a very accepting, open-minded musical atmosphere that encouraged originality."

Welcome to Flat City

Let me put it this way: Recently, while trotting through the Nashville International Airport, I was welcomed to the city by pre-recorded greetings from various country music stars. I didn't catch all of their names, but the script went something like this: "Hey there, I'm Kenny Chesney, and I'd like to welcome you to Music City!" Fair enough. Nashville is the epicenter of country music. Maybe. Not really. Okay, there was a style of country music distinct enough to be called "The Nashville Sound." The city has a serious history. And then there's the business of it all, and *that* is what feeds the branded, local government-sanctioned, nothing-but-the-good-parts version of a city's music scene—which is to say, the version with gobs of money behind it, the version that travels well, that *sells*. On the other hand, there's a more complex reality in Nashville's and every other city's music community that you can only understand once you're on the ground, in the clubs, hearing the music in person, playing it, making it happen, i.e., living it. Try to brand that and you'll lose all the complexity, everything that's good.

Here on the ground in Columbus, I can't help but understand the city's music through my own experiences as a musician. In these flashes of memory, the setting is always night. At sundown you load up the gear, haul it to a club, unload it. Learn the sound person's name. People are smoking outside on the sidewalk in the heat or the rain or the cold. Standard rock 'n' roll time is ten o' clock. The club might be empty or half-full, but it's always a box of shadows. The stage lights are tiny moons. If you play out enough, your circadian rhythms start to adapt. You give up the day for the night. You load out at three in the morning. You drive home under street lamps the color of cantaloupe. This is a flat city, a square inside a circle of highway. It's hard to get lost.

How do you brand that?

I think of a noise show at Bourbon Street, too, fifteen people gathered around a dude in a t-shirt pulling alien screams from his rig.

Gil Mantera's Party Dream in their underwear on the Comfest Main Stage in the thick of the summer.

Jazz combos packed onto the stage at Dick's Den, the neon sign that reads: WHY NOT?

Standing stage-left at a parking lot show while Scrawl plays "Charles."

Driving down from college, a twenty-year-old twit, to see R. C. Mob at the Newport.

Hearing Sharon Udoh of Counterfeit Madison sing for the first time.

The Goldsberrys at Rambling House, my buddy Eric leaning in over a condenser mic.

After-parties and too much whiskey and someone playing a Guinea Worms album.

A night at Little Brothers when Tim Easton was playing "Rewind," and a stranger told me, out of the blue, that it was her favorite song. Then she added, "All my favorite songs are about terrible relationships."

I think of Jim Shepard and his band V-3's vicious, perfect 1996 album, *Photograph Burns*, released on Onion Records, and how it was his final ascent to the big time, and how it didn't go anywhere, and how he hanged himself in 1998.

I was thinking about him, even though I never knew him, the night I went to see his contemporaries Screaming Urge play their "final reunion show" at Carabar in 2011. At the end of the set the band held out the last chords of "Hemophilia/Noise." As Myke Rock flicked his hands across his bass and Mike Ravage readied an acoustic guitar for its destruction, Dave Manic kept pounding away at his kit, shirtless, his chest a thicket of hair, his stomach in tight rolls, his forehead shining, looking not unlike a school principal unleashed for the weekend. The beat took on a uniformity, tribal and hypnotic. Ravage blew up the acoustic guitar and silly string arced into the air. Rock was already offstage. Manic hit what seemed to be the final shot, paused as the audience cheered, then picked up his sticks and went back to it. Rim shots, crashes, thunder—he wouldn't, or couldn't, stop.

The Columbus Sound

There is no Columbus sound. There's a city, and the city you hear depends on the musicians you're listening to. In the 1990s, when the major record labels came a-calling, Thomas Jefferson Slave Apartments' *Bait and Switch* exposed Columbus as a town full of losers, sycophants, and rockers too smart for their own good inside a nation gone stupid. Scrawl, fronted by Marcy Mays and Sue Harshe, turned Columbus into a city of thirty-somethings who were living on the knife's edge of need and disappointment; their version of Flat City taught women to measure twice and cut once. By the late 1990s, Columbus was filthy with alt-country bands, but in 2000, Bigfoot's *Dark Old Days* went a step above with its freewheeling, Band-like community of voices and instrumentation. It made Columbus sound like a good place to be. The rapper Blueprint has by himself made Columbus sound like it lives up to the "smartest city in America" label. Lydia Loveless's Columbus, connected though it may be to decades of rock, country, and punk traditions, is her own city of heartbreak and integrity. In the reverb swirl and folk touches of Saintseneca you might hear Columbus in the summer, a lazy utopia of free afternoons and festivals every weekend. Counterfeit Madison's theatrical soul-meets-punk spirit places me downtown in the clubs and the art galleries where my art school students are looking for themselves. Like the Gibson Brothers on . . . *Build a Raft*, these artists have made their own versions of the city.

As Columbus looks ahead, what worries me is not just that we might lose the complexity of the picture. It's that we might become more interested in a scene than a community, and that some version of what's authentic—"authentic Nashville," "authentic Columbus"—will squeeze some people and the music they make out of the picture altogether.

I think of the night my wife and I swayed to Damn the Witch Siren, an electro-pop duo heavy on attitude and danceability. Bobbi Kitten, on guitar and sampler, and keyboardist Z Wolf play self-described "electronic witch rock," which is one way of describing how in the Spacebar they summoned a neon Halloween of acid flashbacks, slasher B-movies, and gender-fluxing pin-up punk kitsch. But what sticks with me is how Damn the Witch Siren created a world so complete that when my wife and I stepped out into the night, we were disappointed that the rest of the world didn't match up. That's the magic of music, the trick it can pull off: it fills you with possibilities that you take to be realities.

By what strange logic would that night and that band not be considered authentically Columbus?

If you make (or made) music in Columbus, you're authentically Columbus. You belong here, and should be counted here, if you want to be.

Can't Last

BELA KOE-KROMPECHER

The area around Ohio State's campus has always attracted artists, provocateurs, and the kind of kid who would easily strap on a guitar regardless of talent. Talent meant very little to the assortment of characters that have inhabited the student housing around the area, houses that generations have lived in, at one point in my life I lived within stumbling distance of apartments that my mother, my father and uncles all lived in through the 1950s–60s. Houses cut up in pieces to put as many students as humanly possible inside, shoehorned into cramped living spaces, with walls as thin as Vaseline, where empty kegs of beer sat in front yards as if they were barrel-chested lawn ornaments—these were the breeding ground of music, painting, and writing for the soul of Columbus. From the early sprouting of the Capsoul label, founded by future Columbus city leader Bill Moss who inhabited the campus area bar with homegrown songwriter Jeff Smith (who continued to visit Larry's until his death in the 1990s), to the idealistic early songs of a young Phil Ochs to the mini-eruption of noisy-punk sounds that stumbled out of local dives like Stache's and Bernie's throughout the 1990s.

Kids flowed down from I-71 from Cleveland, Canton, and Parma, as if propelled to kick the hard-labored jobs of their parents, and they percolated, then fled from the small coal burgs of southern Ohio, escaping the soot of their grandparents and parents. Congealing around the bars and nightclubs, drinking in not just the libations but the ideas and comfort of others who had one thing that held them in common, which were the thin round 12" platters of vinyl that they all seemed to share during high school even though they grew up hundreds of miles apart. These were thin grooves that spit out the sounds of the Ramones, R.E.M., the Buzzcocks, and of course the North Coast sounds of Devo, Pere Ubu, and the Dead Boys. The revelation first came when clutching the speakers, feeling like a lost fifteen-year-old and listening to the sounds that not only sounded so far away from small-town Ohio but also beckoned to the mysteries of New York and the punk rock scene that jelled in CBGB. At the center of a small universe that was not created by space dust but instead by noise, beer, and clumsy bursts of late-night love, was the record store. Itself the bug light that attracted these once far-flung kids into a thirty-foot by twenty-foot space below High Street where records and CDs were shoved in every available space, a veritable audio orgasm for every displaced English major around High Street.

It was here, at Used Kids records, where many of us met and gathered, egging each other on to make music, produce, and put on shows. The DIY aesthetic was alive and flourishing behind the two-inch thick wooden countertop, as primary owner Dan Dow not only was in the blissfully out-of-tune Gibson Brothers but also ran the independent Okra label that put out records by the Gibson Brothers as well as Cincinnati's Ass Ponys and locals Ricky Barnes. On the other end of the counter was the debauched winsome boy, Ron House, who fronted both the catchy underground rock band Great Plains and also later the much bolder Thomas Jefferson Slave Apartments. Running the mail order service for Used Kids was the tall, handsome Mike "amrep" Hummel, who made perhaps the first self-released punk record in Franklin County. Mike had developed into a sort of poncho-wearing shaman who not only continued to make at times highly experimental folky-underground music but came to be known as a master behind the four-track recording machine, mixing several Guided by Voices records as well as an assortment of records on the Philly-based Siltbreeze (whose founder, Tom Lax, was also an Ohio native). Soon, Dan hired myself along with Jerry Wick, a noisy motormouth from Parma who would answer to "Jerry's an Asshole" and founded the punk-infused band Gaunt.

Jerry was as intense a person who ever walked the sidewalks of High Street; it appeared that his nerves were made of fire, and when he performed he would stutter and jump as if those nerves were exploding at millisecond intervals. Some of us are prone to feel everything in a room, a sensitivity that picks up on every nuance that may or may not upset the balance of all who breathe in the air of the close quarters of living life with such desperate awareness. Always present along the nightclubs and bars of Columbus, Jerry could be easily spotted lugging his threadbare Army backpack, stuffed thick with notebooks, pens, and of course records over his shoulder as well as having a never-ending (but always disappearing) cigarette from his mouth. His nervousness caused him to attack his smokes; it was as if he would inhale the cheapest cigarettes in one mouthful, burning from tip to butt in a flash—he would become one with the cigarette. He could be found huddled in one of the corner booths of Larry's or holding court at one of the five bars he frequented or bending his thin body towards the lurching sounds emanating from guitars at the front of the stage of Stache's. When feeling uncorked, Jerry would fling insults and opinions as if he were an electric popcorn popper, generating derision and anger from even his best of friends. He made an odd sort for one with unbridled ambition to make music, fitting in with much of the underground music world that at once yearned for mass acceptance while also revolting against what was perceived as a tool for corporate music. So many of us felt as if we were subconsciously hoping for the acknowledgement from an establishment we so consciously rejected. In the end, perhaps we were wanting to be part of a family that, like so much of our own families, was as busted as the shitty guitars and amps that we played. Jerry loved Kiss and would say, "I want to be as big as Kiss," and at the same time rejected the idea of selling out his music. But in the end when Warner Brothers came calling, on the heels of a manic rush of releases on some of the finest indie-record labels in America (Thrill Jockey, Amphetamine Reptile, Crypt), Jerry signed the dotted line with the torn hope of being recognized.

There were of course others who sailed in the same boat as Gaunt, those who tried to channel every drop of angst, longing, and hope into a few minutes of sound bursts. In some ways Jerry did it in a manner that was perfect in its imperfection: a handsome man but with crooked teeth and a concave chest (that he always kept hidden), clever but prone to speak ridiculous things (such as wanting to ride the subway from Manhattan to Albany to see a girl), and a friend who had a habit of not being friendly on many occasions. This was emblematic of the low-fi and punk sounds bellowing out of High Street throughout the late 80s and 90s, music that was as catchy and tense as anything being made on either coast but was, at times, recorded on busted four-track machines on Radio Shack cassettes on the quick because if you spent too much time on one idea you might miss the other one that would quickly follow, and the operating manual that we lived by was explicit in stating that there were no bad ideas. Jerry lived with most of the New Bomb Turks, who achieved more success by the meager markings we all went by and were more literate in that they would pummel the listener with a force that felt like punches that left people dazed and askew. They lived a few blocks from Used Kids in a duplex that was more of a crash pad for touring musicians than anything resembling housing for studious college students: all four of the Turks were English majors, which made their garage-punk a bit more literate. (One song was titled "Born Toulouse-Lautrec.") Jerry, who had listened to plenty of the Smiths as well as the Saints and

Ramones, was a dropout from Kent State, where he originally went for music but ditched in favor of English and then finally traded in for a meager living eking out a sustenance, churning out three-chord songs, flipping pizzas, and finally schlepping records with many of the intentional dropouts at Used Kids.

The 1990s brought a white-tinged crest of hope atop a wave of cynicism that finally crashed with 9/11. And in the music world, after pockets of tragedy with the suicide of Kurt Cobain and the utter failure of corporate rock to co-opt the fertile underground rock scene, it finally petered to a halt with a digital exclamation point in the form of Napster and electronic streaming. In the insular bubble of High Street, the major label experiment not only broke up bands and the scene with bands such as Scrawl, the Thomas Jefferson Slave Apartments, Watershed, Gaunt, and V-3 getting signed and soon dropped by major labels but also contributed to the early deaths of V-3's Jim Shepard (suicide) and a few years later the tragic death of Jerry Wick in a hit-skip. Jerry had quietly put Gaunt on hiatus after the band was dropped from Warner Brothers, and he worked to pick up the pieces of a dream that was glued together by idealism, alcohol, and a rough-hewn view of the world that tended only to make sense through records spinning on a turntable. The courtship of Gaunt by Warner Brothers was quick, and it was generally taken as a lark by those who were present, namely the band and a few friends along for the ride, which consisted of expensive dinners where the bar tab far exceeded the actual food eaten. One "dinner" took place at the now-shuttered Kahiki, a tiki-themed restaurant that had a waterfall and rain while people ate bland rice dishes and drank insane cocktails that flamed and soon rendered the drinker incapacitated and unawares how shitty the food was but how wonderful the atmosphere was. The dinner was attended by two Warner Brother's reps (none who drank), four band members (one who didn't drink), and a friend of the band. The only food ordered was by the reps, and the rest of the time at the dinner was taken up by trying to drink every fancy cocktail on the menu. Some were served in skull glasses, some in Easter Island statue glasses, and one was served in a large moat-like ceramic dish where people stuck straws in the moat while dry ice-powered fog rose out of the center. The final bill was over $700, and Gaunt was signed to Warner Brothers. Jerry was an easy date.

Jerry wore Converse sneakers, black jeans, and either t-shirts or, later, a variety of western-themed shirts that were easily had for a few bucks at Dollar Thrift or Goodwill in the 90s. It was as easy time to be indiscreet with fashion. Besides, in Columbus nobody really gave a fuck. After signing his deal, Jerry kept things close to his chest, trying to balance the wanting of over ground success that may counter the underground respectability of apathy and isolation. It was one thing to walk around the beach and another to dive into the ocean. While some may think the easiest path to success is through wide acclaim and money, there is a very real sense of losing one's essence by taking a risk. Some of us just chose to keep ourselves afloat with creativity in the world we knew best. After signing, nothing changed with him, his black canvas Chuck Taylors, worn jeans, and thrift store shirts did not blossom into anything designer, and since he didn't have a driver's license there was no new car to drive. His world was Larry's, a home-grown bohemian bar that helped many struggling artists and bar stool philosophers over a fifty-year period feel a part of a community, Stache's, and of course Used Kids. Shortly around this time, he was forced out of his part-time job at Used Kids to concentrate on Gaunt. The demands of touring and recording proved to be too much for the shop that had experienced a financial success that it had never been looking or designed for thanks to the CD revolution.

The making of Gaunt's Warner Brother's debut, "Bricks and Blackouts," was fraught with writer's block and the label's insistence on using a name producer. While the band always had Jerry's final control now, the stakes were higher, as if one were now moving into a well-lit room naked, all perceived flaws could be noticed and nitpicked. In hindsight, it is easy to see that the upper or even middle management at Warner

Brothers did not have Gaunt high on their hopes for a hit. This was a period when bands were being signed like a shopper at a supermarket, things were being pulled off the indie-rock shelves and dumped into the grocery carts of these large labels. Although if someone is one of those things, i.e., product, the plan is to be made into a Thanksgiving dinner and not a throw-away microwavable dinner. There could be the argument that art should be allowed to be made organically, in a person's own petri dish, with all of the ingredients people use to make art their own—smashed up childhoods, love that breathes and then gets choked by its own expectations, the creative impulse to gut all the happiness and pain. Let it live on the page, on a canvas, or on a thin slab of vinyl as the sole purpose of the entire exercise of creation. And then, depending on the masses it may turn into a commodity.

By the end of the 1990s the slim corridor of High Street that stretched from south campus to the north end, a place that started with the punk-ish/new-wave club of Crazy Mama's and ended in the smoke and beer-soaked carpet of Stache's nearly three miles north, had started to change. The building that housed Crazy Mama's was torn apart for the more "acceptable" South Campus Gateway of mobile phone shops, chain restaurants, and sports bars, and as the university's version of gentrification inched forward, other ingredients fell by the wayside in the name of progress. Stache's closed shop in 1999, as the landlord would not renew the lease and would transform into Little Brothers in the Short North until limping into its closing in the mid-aughts. Gaunt was dropped from Warner Brothers in early 2000. The indie-rock experiment of the major labels had for the most part been a disaster for many bands and musicians. It was a boon to some (Green Day, Soundgarden, and Pearl Jam) but left the carcasses of many bands in its wake including Gaunt, V-3, and most other Ohio bands in that grand money-grab. Jerry quickly found a new calling that he was passionate about, which was cooking. He got a job as a chef in a Short North pub and bought a small house on the other side of I-71, just a few miles from campus.

He rode his bike daily from his small post-war ranch house to campus and work nearly every day. He made songs in his basement and slowly started to break through the shattered expectations of the major label. We all wanna be famous if just to be eternal. Late one night in early 2001 while riding his bike home after a night of drinking Jerry was struck down by a hit and run driver and died just blocks from Stache's, his neck shattered as he lay on the side of the road. Later that year, during the hottest days of summer, a shoddy electrical outlet finally quit trying and a fire consumed Used Kids, not just burning up the music but also lighting thousands of memories to the sky. Jenny Mae then moved to Florida, never to make another record, and over the next ten years, the powers that be bulldozed the campus area by slow degree. Bernie's was torn apart by a wrecking ball to make way for mixed-use housing, Larry's was sold and shuttered, only to be transformed into a chain burrito store—one could argue nobody has ever met their future spouse in this new inhabitant, while no doubt many generations found their first spark in the chunky wooden booths of Larry's (including my mother and father). There is something to be found in looking over one's shoulder while trodding forward with metaphysical tattered Chuck Taylor's, but in the end, what made something special for a brief, exploding moment can't last—nor should it.

COLUMBUS, OHIO

BILLY IRELAND CARTOON LIBRARY

IF I stand here long enough somebody will come look at my art—

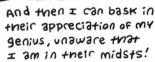

And then I can bask in their appreciation of my genius, unaware that I am in their midsts!

Huh.

Ah, here's someone now.

What do you think? Good stuff, right? My favorite!

?

...are you the artist of this page?

What? No way! Not me!

Sheesh! How embarrassing! I'm out of here!

I'll walk it off.

Perfect weather!

It's surprising how quickly this city felt like home to me.

Maybe it has something to do with being a cartoonist... what is it about cartoonists and Ohio? It's been the cradle of some of the best artists in this medium!

Even now I'm walking upon the very same land that was once trod upon by James Thurber and Milton Caniff!

In the Silent City
She's Yearned For

JEN TOWN

She'll find herself here, in the silent city
she's yearned for, touching its sooty surfaces
while its students of argyle and innocence
traipse along, toting their heavy bags. Under the pavement,
 pavement,
and under the dirt, bones, the silt of ancient rivers.
She's standing on the centuries. She's standing in someone's
small village. She'll never be alone here. The children
walk by with their Italian ices,
the wind smells of exhaust, of baking bread. With night com-
 ing on,
where will she go? The park is full of the homeless,
the shops on High have closed. Her apartment,
its light burning, seems to belong to someone else.
She'll look into her own window, press her nose
to the warmth. A stranger walks by,
talking into his hand, promises I'll look for you.
But, mister, how will you know who you've found?

Cactus

JEN TOWN

I've named him Albert
the name I give plants,
as good as any other, and talk to him
because I talk to everything
in this domestic world: the cat, the cast-iron
skillet, the dust motes shifting down
through sunlight. Does this space need
the lace of my words?
Albert once had the shape of a man:
a torso, two fat arms,
a small budding head until he grew
out of this form, though to me,
he's still homunculus. In his green pot,
a small stick collected from Lake Erie
and a plastic cat that looks up
the height of him, startled, and—
Surprise! Another cat, buried up to the neck
like this is a feline Western
and the one cat, a villain
in the manner of mustache-twirling
has buried our hero under a cactus
where red ants nip away at him.
Will our hero escape? Will the other cat ride off
into the sunset that is the dining room light
that due to a faulty switch,
begins to flicker on and off

like the glorious sky out west,
so huge one can see
one's face reflected
like a mirror, like a god?
When it rains in this Western, the cats
stare up, their stupid faces wet.
They can't imagine a way out.

Diorama Turned to Ashes

JEN TOWN

for Drake Dutton

The walls, once painted
with ferns, have burned. What's left
but a few charcoal wisps
smudged by a boy's small fingers,
a plastic tree taken from
an unrelated toy set, melted
like a coin of green gum,
stuck to the cardboard ground,
and, here, the anachronism
of people, plastic figures
covered in ash, deformed
but still human: a man and woman
walk toward where once
the tyrannosaurus waved
his tiny arms, as if
beckoning them into the future.
What a strange world we've imagined
for ourselves and then, once built,
set upon. Picture it whole again, little peephole
through which flora and fauna
live out their fraught existence—
in the distance a looming
match brightens the sky.

Black Woman Repetition
(*After Terrance Hayes*)

BARBARA FANT

Black woman, college degree
Black woman, masters
Black woman student loans,

Black woman loaned her life over to student,
Student, Black woman, woman full time job

Single black woman over 30
Single black woman . . . 30?

Black woman, world calls bitter
Black woman bitten angry black,
Black woman bitter black angry broke
Is she the only thing broken?

Let's talk about war, let's talk about Vietnam men coming home
  limbless,
Agent orange where black souls should be,

Let's talk about fathers, daddy didn't come home,
Black woman got daddy issues, black woman daddy issues,
Black woman, 30 still dealing with daddy issues?

Black woman nurse black man, Black father?
Black boy too afraid of his own insecurities?

Black woman, black hole
Black woman not whole?

Black woman, black woman, you are more than just the hole
  your thighs uphold

Woman of black, Black woman you are not always the night,
you are not always black and blue,

Black woman not Jonah,
Black boy, are you Jonah?
What do you do when there's fear inside you the size of a
  whale's body?

Black woman wail, Black woman travail for black man,
black woman pray, black woman pray, black woman, don't be
  another man's prey

She swim, black woman float, woman water,
Black woman your face not always an aquarium's explosion

Magic Before/Before Magic

BARBARA FANT

We have been called magic before,
Our eyes, subtle stillness, dancing to the branches of our bodies,
Our bodies
tree limbs reaching towards Heavens,
above the sun,
above the rain
dance rivering us out of our bones,

We have been called magic before,
Swinging from trees until we became them,
Bearing the fruit of someone else's child,
nursing someone else's child while ours lay hanging,
its body, a box of bones we're forced to carry six feet beneath
  our chests,
So we dig deep
inside our bodies and pull out every ounce of glittered prayer
  glistening
until it reaches our tongues and we learn to speak life over
  ourselves,

We have been this magic before,
Bursting into everyone else's box of glitter and shine
and hiding the fact that we birthed it,
it came from our womb,
we lay bruised and bloodied while they dance into midnight
until they become the stars we own,
We do own the stars, ya know,

We have been that magic before,
How else could you find something to wish upon in this shade
  of midnight
if it didn't already come sulked in our skin's shade of brilliant,

We have been this magic before
Teaching the moon to dance and bend her dust into the shape
  of an eye,
peering out onto everyone's breath while they sleep
to make sure they keep breathing through every ounce of night
  that hits their lives,

Like,
My magic is so black,
she looked in the mirror and called herself solar system
My magic is so black,
the stardust grew herself a fro,
braided her body into cornrows
My magic is so black,
she bounced her reflection off the ocean and the waves started
  sea-walking
My magic is so black,
her midnight's blues mistook her throat for hip hop, and jazz,
  and poetry, and mystery, and religion, and art, and culture,
and culture,
and culture,
everything stolen from her body's magic in the first place,

Where culture was ripped from our veins,
we learned to river ourselves into a chandelier of cardinals
  taking flight,
cutting the sky into red until everyone learned
how to bleed the rhythm of this nation,
We are the rhythm of this nation,
In all its black and brownness,

Black history is American history,
America does not exist without this hue of sand
and wood and tornado, and casket
We have learned to carve the caskets from our own bodies
and sing a new song louder,
carved the caskets from our throats
and bloomed a new tongue,
There is always a new tongue to be bloomed,

And we have always been this magic,
We have been called this wishbone and golden before,
But when they forget our names,
and they will,
because they do, often,
Every ounce of glitter left in our bodies will rise into a new
 body,
And throat,
And tongue,
Until we braid ourselves into a new language again,
Rewrite history again,
In all that magic
And rise,
And rise, and
Rise

Long Line of Strong Women

BARBARA FANT

I come from a long line of strong women
Who know how to birth, and load rifles all at the same time
Who juggle babies and careers and swallowed whole every
 man that ever raised his fist
I think of fist, I think of woman,
The unclenched skin of a toothless hand
When he opened his hand and showed me her teeth,
I remember the powerlessness,
How my throat would never sing this song again,
I remember the wedding day, how somehow Mrs. made it feel
 like woman,
And then the surgery,
And the house I was thrown out of,
The bruises that bloomed on my body in the morning,
When I say, I come from a long line of strong women,
I mean, I come from fire-breathers,
Which means, I come from dragons,
Which means, I come from beings that slay
There is no gun to erase you here
These, are not daddy issues,
Not my brokenness,
This is a fist,
Torched the air with every fiber,
A slice through the sky
Middle finger and ring finger all side by side,
When I say, I come from a long line of strong women,

What I mean is, I died a thousand times,
And I always come back
Alive

Transplant

FAYCE HAMMOND

It's the first day of real sunlight
since the winter laid its hands
across the Midwest's eyes,
and my therapist coddles a cup of tea
across from me, the mouth
of the mug breathing ghosts
like I did last week.

He makes a joke about the weather,
says he put in a good word for me.
I laugh, like his tea
wish I could be held. The couch shrinks
around me and that's close enough.

Where's home? Along the foothills
of the Wasatch mountains.
The high desert. Wherever
my love is. *Where are you?* Not
there. Never there. *Where's your love?*
I don't know. I never know.

He asks again. *Where's home?*
Where the roots are. It's funny.
I'm here because I couldn't put down roots.
I'm here because I can't transplant.

He asks if I'm stuck in the desert
somewhere. *Yes.* He asks if the desert
wants me to stay there. *Yes.* He asks
if I owe the desert my loyalty. *Yes.*
He asks if I think the desert stops me

from learning how to be
somewhere else. *Of course.*
He does not ask
if I should break up with the desert.
We both know the answer.

I mention how sunny it is back home,
even in the winter. I taste like ghosts.
He empties his cup of tea, kindly
says nothing more.

Fear of Fuel

FAYCE HAMMOND

A low tire had me squatting
next to an air pump
at some Columbus gas station,
fumbling with the gauge,
hose coiled around one thigh
taut against the hem
of my favorite pair of short shorts.

It's this new city and I've never known humid.
I don't like melting out
like this. I could ignore Utah's heat
and keep my skin covered,
but here, here I am
counting the seconds to my car's AC insides

until some shadow eclipses me. *I can fill that for you.*
A man, the most mountain thing in this city,
and my hands slip on the gauge.
No, thank you. Smile. I'm almost done.
But he doesn't leave and his eyes grin

the serrated edge of a knife
and I feel them catching
on the meat of my thighs, hungry,
and I am thankful for the billow in my top
but I wish I would melt faster.

He is more persistent than humidity,
stickier, too, his razor eyes
carving into my curve
and I'm not sure how I got him to leave
me alone, but I swallowed so much tremble
and lied about a boyfriend
and somehow ended up
on an unfamiliar neighborhood street
and cried on the phone
to some girl who gave me a drink
and her number just last Monday
and I've only been in this city
for three goddamn weeks
and I've been filleted open

and this has never happened before.
I know I'm supposed to be a good fat girl
and be grateful for the butchering
because in Salt Lake City, my body was invisibility.
A specter eyes slid off and away from
unless my hand was in my girl's hand
and we were too close
to a Church corner.

My body has never been safe
but I'm not sure which is the best way to bleed.
Bitten open by hungry mouths craving a feast
or chewed by hateful teeth raging for a kill,
my wounds gape the same way.

I am still afraid of gas stations.

Main Street

ROSE M. SMITH

Who do we indict for this
slow murder?
For the closed eyes
of thriving proprietorships
for weathered wood, tattered posts,
spray painted ensigns. Like locusts,
starved and foraging, we
have torn to boarded barrenness
the inner city heart—storefronts,
aging private homes, empty shells
of restaurants waiting to be filled.
While Wexner sprawl, Glimcher span
and commerce rule, each a hungry babe
centered only on its longing, suck
life from the flaccid breast of State & High,
leaving empty flow where city life had been,
walls where windows once looked out
onto clots of culture clinging to the vein.
We love this violation, hold it like a lover,
send our dollars out to all their pretty places—
outskirts, suburbs, monuments to millions.
Mom-and-Pops abandoned for new-fashioned
elite when a knife turned on the heart
might have saved us all the trouble.

Billboard, 2013

ROSE M. SMITH

Sexuality . . . one of the most powerful tools of marketing.
—Anonymous

At Broad & James her 36 Triple Ds loom
round and full above Shell station pumps. We wait
for green, for go.

99.7, The Blitz, new rock, embroidered on her
front, the headless torso promises
when you tune in

she'll reveal the ample buoyancy
this station holds. Slim fingers frame her shelf
as if to shield the food of infant nations

from wind, howl, insidious engine whine.
Pray for rain, the sign commands.
Wet tee-shirt moments beckon

while eastbound men, distracted at the light,
bow their heads as others' heads rise
beneath her manicured hands.

Ackerman Place

PSYCHE NORTH TOROK

The women, dressed in their business
suits and hose
don white sneakers for a lunchtime
walk.

Their hair is perfect, a perfect match
for white sneakers.
They don't go out alone.
Now or ever.
They walk in groups of two or three,
the coiffured women.
It is a warm day without any
rain.

They power-walk, they power-walk,
they talk they talk they talk.
Such critical
conversation in their days;
significance in those hose, in
pristine sneakers.

They walk across
the pavement the pavement the pavement.
They do not touch
the grass, the twigs, the leaves.

They do not touch.

Nighthawks

(Buckeye Donuts)

JOSEPH HESS

Smoke from the burning doughnut oil
infuses with the lonely

post-game colognes lining the formica
counter at the High Street

haunt simmering in the late night.
Here, austere decades have passed

gazing into bottomless graying
porcelain cups, and now I think

she knows her own secret loss.
Let's not be specific. All our stories

subscribe to straighter lines
past old lovers, but privately

we know we're not always
who we should be, which hinders

my breath. Subversive love
is wedged between what never was

and what will always be. Silence
is the black night beyond

the glass panes reflecting patrons
that blur into my lines of age,

I fear truer than any hope
I still rent in our room upstairs.

American Folklore

ADAM J. GELLINGS

I got a knock on the front door the other day from an elderly
 man
    & his wife
the man said he had a question if I didn't mind
    I said I didn't mind what was the question
he asked what I knew about the family murdered in that house
    over there
    at the end of the cul-de-sac
    years ago
I followed his boney finger, callused knuckle
I said when we were kids we called it the murder house
    my father had helped build it
I said his name was written in white chalk on one of the beams
    in the attic
    along with the other four that helped
    it's probably still there actually
I said I remembered the wife's name was Louisa
    she was a nurse but always wanted to be an actress
    one year I watched the Sugar Bowl in the living room with
    the kids
I said that Florida State quarterback sure threw all over the
 Buckeye defense
    that night
I remembered the dad had a lot of books in the den
My dad helped nail plywood on all the windows afterward
    I bet those panels wished they were still trees

as you can see
    the shutters are all rotted
We used to throw the baseball over there
    it was messy
    it was real messy
I said rampage
    no I didn't but my old man did
    when he came back home he said he needed to sit down
    hysterical
    all three kids the wife the husband the nanny
I said it was the wife's coworker at the hospital
    yep sure was
I said flesh
    who knows why
    just sits there like an abandoned prayer
I said yep that's the murder house
    cars pass by it slowly
    three bedrooms two & a half baths.

The Whales Are Always Feeding

ETHAN RIVERA

After the whales say *I do*, the church whirlpools
applause for another mass wedding. We

plankton were invited, or perhaps
pushed, to witness this union. From above

the veneer of ocean, we coexist. In this body
of water, we are numerous. We are a flood of

names. Believe in a god so mercilessly,
it emerges into a dryer heaven. The current hustles

us to the reception where we hope to dance
and expose ourselves a masterpiece.

Body full of worth. This has always been
our current. To be noticed

in a food chain that defines us edible.
We are our own reckoning, pounding our feet

into possibility. We are vast, if only they could
see us smile. When the whales open

their mouths, gun barrel hungry,
what are we but delusions of grandeur? Small

promises waiting to be loved or eaten.
What is the whale other than a death we always expected

to call home? Even on a day where they promise entire forevers
to each other, they cannot promise us our lives. Only questions

of our ancestors and what we have done to deserve
here. To not become

the meal they can rationalize
again and again.

Justice Be Like

ETHAN RIVERA

On the same day six cops in Baltimore
were told they hadn't gotten away
with it yet, a warehouse blew up

on the south side of Columbus,
while protesters, on the other side of town,
marched peacefully in challenge of another headstone.

I watched the smoke billowing,
turning the sky so black
I wondered which camera would call it a riot first.

If you are too silent,
the wind can
take away your name.

But if you are too loud
and a warehouse should explode
when you say justice,

they do not ask questions.
They point and tell
everyone it's your fault.

Because asking nicely entails
whispering it, so they can pretend,
they didn't hear you.

Shapes Heard Free

DARREN DEMAREE

There is a muscle
dark enough
to be considered forest

in the middle of the city
that has no desire
to be a city

& that thick tether
that wraps around
our shallow rivers

is made of fox
hearts that beat
with the hope

of every veined heart,
with the hope
that if we can all move

fast enough we will
see a people with
the deer

& with each other
& blurred just enough
to become the shapes

heard free by the rest
of Ohio, by the nature
of Ohio, by the anger

calming into a focus
that can create enough
path to widen Ohio

into a home that rises
above the cold shale
we were born on.

Do the Right Thing

CHARLENE FIX

The night before the march on the Statehouse
to encourage Ohio's electors to climb a mountain
of reason, I had a dream.

I was sitting in a circle of film buffs with Spike Lee!
He asked if anyone had something to say. "I do! I do!"
I cried, waving my hand,

then was off to the races, unable to restrain my flow
on beloved films from all over the world, my words
pouring from such depths

they fairly echoed. What films? What did I say
about them? Nothing remains, only the felt intensity,
joined to the suspicion

that I was talking way too much and would benefit
more from listening, in addition to Lee's patient
countenance as he turned

halfway away to gaze into the distance. Similarly,
decades ago, I found myself seated at a small round
table with W. H. Auden

soon after I began to write again. In that Dick Cavett
setting we talked about poetics and poems all night,
the bliss of it remaining

though our words dissolved the moment I wakened.
In both dreams my soul was rent, my words were water
streaming from a gouged glass.

Two hundred of us marched around the Ohio Statehouse
on the nineteenth of December 2016, a bright cold day,
mostly in a loop before

the east façade, the side the sun rises on, the direction
we Jews gravitate to in cities, and Muslims kneel
to speak with God,

and where the hoped-for Hamilton Electors would enter,
marchers with bullhorns leading us in rhymed chants,
one ending with "do the right thing,"

while cameras recorded us, and the telltale lambs' wool
top-coats of the powerful darkly swayed. For them,
the "right thing" was mistaken

for the wrong thing, the thing we were there to prevent
in this bitterly ironic age, for the electors failed to apprehend
the spirit of civic duty.

The lessons of great films and poems might have cracked
open the seals on their hearts, which may be why
Lee and Auden

let this novitiate yak the night away, Auden, who revealed
our mortar of Eros and of dust, its urgent flame,
and Lee, who

embedded an imperative phrase into the culture,
one the electors didn't know to know, so kicked it
away like a can.

Ornithology

GEOFF ANDERSON

Locked out, I found a feather on my porch,
ran its fibers down my life line. Holding it in my hand
was the closest I ever came to wings. My finger traced
its white circles surrounded by a black colder than night.
If I were an animal, I'd be a woodpecker, the complexion
of my parents. It was the season of awakening,
beaks living not on bark, but what they found inside.
Taps dug deeper in the birch around me, not even the heart
safe from the hunt. But what color is a bird?
I had no answer for what one looked like naked—
the pink of morning; the rainbow of oil on the street;
me, still pale in May. There is hunger in asking
if anyone is there behind the wood. I caught my hand
knocking on my door in unison with the drumming.
If I were a woodpecker, would I see the pattern as a song,
or my feathers as my skin, or myself staring back in the glass?

Phasmophobia

GEOFF ANDERSON

After Jamaal May

The girls are back to double dutch.
Home for Easter, I watch each length
of string, the clap of cable in mom's
parking spot, a foot snagged, a new game
whipping the road again. I have never
jumped rope. It is familiar the way
family I'll never meet is familiar.
Their names are served with seconds
of cornbread at the dinner table.
Strange how endings twist themselves;
seeing the rope knotted on the sidewalk
when they finish, the first verb I think of
is hang. What do I know about gravity?
In college, I did not hear my first
ghost story, just the one I can remember.
A student made a pendulum out of a
rope and the clothes rod in his closet.
The power turns on by itself at night
in the dorm room where he was
found. It could have been me
waking up to a burst of light.
Last night, my dad flipped
the switch on in my room.
Sorry. He forgot I was there.

If I were a ghost, what else would
be forgotten? I haven't considered
my name will lose its meaning,
the number of generations
between me and the thought,
my mom saying this is the room
where I used to sleep.

Flyover Country

STEVE ABBOTT

You'd think it's the middle of an old mattress,
a low spot downhill from those resilient edges
where everything sits, better by some reckoning
that finds a crust more tasteful than the bread.
The middle, though, quietly indicts the absence
of imagination revealed in how movies and TV
use *Ohio* or *Iowa* as code word, a shorthand
slur to suggest the pitifully unhip who suffer
a gee-whiz form of innocence mixed with a lack
of broadband, cell phones, any form of ecstasy.
Not to mention this season's shoes, detachment,
designer drugs and sex—all the staples of life.

Cities sprout from the high corn and wheat,
with bodegas, good pastrami, sweaty nightclubs.
Streets babble syllables that have crawled halfway
around the world to land in kitchens and boardrooms.
Bass beats slug it out with brass-knuckle rock 'n' roll
in the blue shadows diagrammed by bright lights
and architecture that redefines the concept of landscape.
Dancing between the great mountain ranges are
boutiques, limousines, black-tie galas and poetry
venues that some nights smoke even the trendy
hangouts of the Lower East Side or North Beach.
And immigrant cabbies in rush-hour gridlock.

Here, we too smack our children breathless
and shrug as bailiffs heap a neighbor's couches
and clothing at the curb. Our galleries match anything
slapped on canvas by the Nouveau Grotesque school
of post-modernism, and who cares if we snort
a terminal irony every bit as lethal as meth?
Explosions of liquor and gunfire? S&M? We've got it.
And kids, even rich ones, put needles in their arms.
Just like the coasts, regardless of weather,
we stride past layers of coats on the invisible form
holding a cup quarters sometimes ring into,
sights and soundtracks every bit as stirring and
current as anything on the checklist of Cool.

Hold Me Like Ohio

AMY TURN SHARP

My child came to me last night
and he held me like Ohio
like the river I swam in
like the hills I climbed
the old state fairground
trees sketched against the sky
like a goddamn country song
he held me like Ohio
till the windows weren't black
till my body became a bridge
that took him
to the other side
of sleep
to a place
he felt free
and I rocked him like Ohio
because that's what I was born to do
there are places we live
and places that live within us
like fully expressed ideas
perfectly constructed thoughts
like love

Summertime

ROBERT COLBY

I was surprised when I saw the ragtag company careening

Like a band of children in early films of city streets

Back when cities were teeming

I watched as they rolled down the path between the sky-
scrapers

Charged up a small flight of stairs to a locked back door

Dusted with summer and sweat

Not a grown-up in sight

Calmly I asked them what they were doing

"We at the library" one of them said proudly

I laughed

The library was three blocks away

The others turned to me and smiled too

I figured they were on the lam and somewhere a grown-up
 was frantically counting heads

For half a second I looked at them across the threshold

For half a second I was part of their caper

I walked away and the little world closed behind me

Walking in the Topiary Park
After Snowfall in February

JEREMY GLAZIER

First snow came late this winter,
a white blind suddenly dropped over
these women and men who've made do with only the cover
of a parasol all winter; a monkey; a pipe. Last year,
                                        November
brought out brushes and shovels:
I saw cars stuck for days downtown in drift, swirls
of spun-out tire tracks long before the calendar unfurled
its garlands and carols.

The snow
has no business invading the Grande Jatte here, now,
Seurat's little green beach so deep into the new year.
                                        No
right or reason
except to remind us we are only points, each alone
in a landscape, and sooner or later this will all be done and
  gone.

On the First Snowfall

WILL EVANS

my daughter begs me to play outside and so we wrapped our-
selves in every shield we could find its two degrees outside
and no fun can be had from blackened fingertips. I try to tell
her about the frostbite that took her great-grandfather's fingers
and made him left handed, but she never met that dude so
she basically says whatever we're in the snow for twenty min-
utes which might as well be generations and when I tell her
we've lost enough heat to never truly be the same, she dunks
her face into the only un-trampled patch of yard we have left
and comes up for air, a fallen night worth of frost on her face.
Doesn't my beard make me look older daddy and of course she
doesn't look older but she does look less mine then she did a
moment ago and since this is what getting older means, then
I say *yes love* before she disappears into the wind or until an-
other snowfall lingers longer than we deserve.

Auribus Teneo Lupum

WILL EVANS

The archway above
the door of my daughter's new
school says something in Latin
about hard
work and leadership
but nothing about the tuition
fee required to walk through it.
The school is only new to us
as it has stood without us or people
that look like us
for decades,
and this is what my wife and I do
with our hard work and leadership;
a ransom we have secured,
we grease the rails for our daughter.
This is what you do
when you
are Black
and at jobs where you
suffer
through being
the minority,
you send your daughter
to the better
school where she
will suffer through being

the minority. But they love us
here. They love the shirt
and tie I pick as armor
to wear when I leave my daughter
with them. They love locks that twist
down my wife's back
like taut rope they can point
out to investors. Your family is adorable,
would you mind posing
for this picture, you know we are remaking
the flyer, can we put you on the cover?
Give us
your daughter, she was too smart
to stay wherever
you came from. See the community
we're building? See how
we have tamed the wild
dogs, I bet you haven't heard
one bark since you got here. We can't
guarantee they won't get
hungry if you leave.

The New Oath

HANNAH STEPHENSON

If a child is in pain, let us help that child.
If a child is in our vicinity, let us not harm that child.
If a child is black. A boy. Neither. Let us help that child.
If a child is at the bus stop
leaving childhood for teenagerdom
or a toddler in a backseat, let us not harm that child.
If a child shares our citizenship or does not.
If a child has done wrong, let us help that child.
If a child is playing with his sister, let us not harm that child.
If a child has behaved like a child, let us help that child.
If a child is pretending to be an adult,
let us not harm that child
and if a human is helpless before us, let us
remember how easily broken or harmed
they are, let us remember the baby they were
as their parents gathered them up in their arms, let us remember
the children they love or might go on to love
if we shield them if we guide them.
Let us remember we are made of
slender bone and stretched, soft flesh.
If if if. When when when.
Amen.

Table Manners

FARIHA TAYYAB

In my culture, we do not have table manners. This is the response
for my student after reading about a Chinese boy having tea with
Englishmen.

Young blood—
You may not have a table,
but you have table manners.

You may not have silverware
but you have mastered God's utensils.

You may not have a large saucer for cookies
but your tea is suffice to turn someone's day around.

You may not have dinner napkins
but your immunity speaks to your hygiene.

You may have one large plate,
but your communities don't suffer from isolation.

You may serve yourself when you wish,
but your generosity has always filled bellies.

You may come from poverty,
but you treat your guests like royalty

You may be embarrassed by your cuisine
in the white man's land,
but young blood,
when they love themselves,
they will come to realize they stole the table from you.

Thanksgiving

FARIHA TAYYAB

My daughters dance,
white heels of her feet on Red earth.
Her feet now a crimson brown, from clay
So pure and so protected.

Different from the stories of men with white feet,
and the same white soles that possessed this land.
How do I tell her the home that she loves has been stolen?
That the people that roamed were murdered then enslaved
and if not enslaved then put in prison.
Real prisons like cages where even animals don't belong.
These are the stories of the forefathers.
And we are as American inheriting them from one land to
   another.
Migrating from one stolen land to another.

This story is different,
The colonizers did not leave, they remained on this red soil
And when they had guilt, they created Thanksgiving
and made false images, of corn on the cob, and
indigenous crowns
So we do not know how to interact with our mother
Oh, this earth, that gave us life.
Who provided our own mothers with an earthquake
to release the flood of life from her womb that birthed us.

The Dead Walk Over Your Land

RUTH AWAD

But first the flood came. And the animals drowned by the
  hundreds,
paddled and reached until they were too tired to keep their
  mouths
above water. And their lungs burned, first with exhaust and
  then
with water. And God looked down and affirmed what your
grandmother always said: *Animals don't go to heaven.*

Fine. But we're above water now.
And the land hums with its own desires:
north. You're imagining the glasses your mother
pulled down from the cabinet. Or she's at the foot
of your bed, the weight of her.

But now the vines reclaim the windows.
Your cabinets open, dishes exposed like teeth.
A wound, exhumed, and the animals
are swimming, your mother is walking,
they are all home, they are all with you.

Inventory of What Remains

RUTH AWAD

The unmade bed,
sheets coiled
like the end of a rope.

Lip-print sealing
the rim of the glass
you last sipped.

The door sighing
open when the furnace
thrums.

Robins like a heartbeat
behind the shrub.

My hands tracing
slats of sunlight,
their impartial divide:
mine, yours.

I know at least
what love feels like,
don't tell me I don't.

Taillights

RUTH AWAD

Gauzy moonlight
snagged in the window.
My mother's
georgette sleeves.

Outside the highway grits,
cars panting through the dark,
grazing all night—
asphalt for field,
miles of want—

exhaust
slung over the power lines
like one old coat
in a closet full of empty hangers.

Some Friday

ANDREW ANDERSON

And there will come a day when you will open your mouth and out will come your mother or father, or some distant relative you did not know you held within you and you will be surprised enough you may just miss your turn, or put that dish down hard enough to chip it, or mow right into a bed of lavender. If you haven't already been wearing a seatbelt, it will then be time to reconsider. The butcher block countertops will be a nice addition. You never really liked your landscaping the way it was. This is why you must have more dishes than you think you need. Family always comes home one way or another.

Acknowledgments

I would like to express a giant, great big, all-encompassing THANKS to all the Columbus writers who have been so incredibly generous, introducing me to other incredible writers and answering my urgent emails when I send them. The Columbus literary community is truly worth celebrating.

I want to take a moment and acknowledge the writers of Columbus who are focusing on fiction. We didn't include fiction in this anthology for various reasons, but I know there are extraordinary writers in town doing the work.

Thanks to the Flyover Fest team for creating a festival that celebrates independent artists in Flyover Country. The book fair alone is a treat, but the programming is a testament to both your eye and your sense of community. It was at your inaugural book fair that I met Anne Trubek, and that's where this anthology came to life.

Thank you, Anne Trubek, for starting Belt Publishing and the city anthologies. From a gal who loves to read about what makes a place distinct, having the collected work of the writers in each city is a magnificent gift that I'm truly grateful to read.

I would also like to thank Jill Moorhead for cooking up the idea for a collection of books by and about Midwestern writers, and Justin Johnston for his encouragement and support as we launched and developed the Flyover Library at Wild Goose Creative. I also want to thank Jasmine Barfield for her glorious work that got us the grant to give it life. I appreciated the opportunity to serve authors in our community through the project, and I look forward to future iterations as the library grows in new hands.

Thank you to the booksellers and baristas who are absolutely essential in fueling the literary life of our fair city. I want to make a special shout out to Charlie Pugsley from Bookspace Columbus for always always curating a remarkable selection, and talking books with such patience and grace.

Many thanks to Tony Sanfilippo and Debra Jul at The Ohio State University Press for their guidance, patience, and expertise as we brought this thing to life.

And finally, a big shout out to the steadfast friends this gal wouldn't want to be without: Lauren, Paula, Sarah, Chrissie, Jen, Emily, Nikole, Samantha, David, Debbie, Patty, Mary, Kim, Kimberly, Lori, Neal, Darrell, Nicole B., Nicole E., Pete, Ehling, Kilgore, and Jones (I'm stopping here because the list is long), and special thanks to Claressa Page because, as you know, *we're related*. Also, thank you John, Debbie, David, Brodie, and Wes. I got a good fam.

The following pieces featured in this anthology appeared previously in the publications noted.

"In a City Marked by Change, Columbus Crew SC Remains a Powerful, Unifying Force" by Hanif Abdurraqib was previously published in MLS Soccer in December 2015.

"Columbus" by Maggie Smith was previously published in Buzzfeed News in October 2017.

"The New Oath" by Hannah Stephenson was previously published in her chapbook, *Cadence*, winner of the Ohio Chapbook Prize from the Wick Poetry Center (Kent State University Press, 2018).

"The Blue Jackets Have Turned Columbus into a Major League City" by Jeff Svoboda was previously published in 1st Ohio Battery in April 2017.

"Art in a City That Can Kill You" by Scott Woods was previously published on his website, Scott Woods Writes Lists, in March 2017.

"Five Reasons Why Writers Should Move to Columbus" by Annie McGreevy was previously published on LitHub in August 2016.

"In the Silent City She Yearned For" by Jen Town was previously published in her collection, *The Light of What Comes After* (Bauhan Publishing, 2018).

"Diorama Turned to Ashes" by Jen Town was previously published in *Sweet: A Literary Confection* in 2018.

"Hold Me Like Ohio" by Amy Turn Sharp was previously published in her collection, *Hold Me Like Ohio*, in 2014.

"American Folklore" by Adam J. Gellings was previously published in *Prelude Magazine* in 2017.

"Ornithology" by Geoff Anderson was previously published in *Flypaper Magazine* in March 2018.

"Phasmophobia" by Geoff Anderson was previously published in *Cold Creek Review* in 2017.

"The Dead Walk Over Your Land" by Ruth Award was previously published in *Southern Indiana Review* in 2014.

"Justice Be Like" by Ethan Rivera was previously published as an audio recording in Us 4 President in July 2017.

"Auribus Teneo Lupum" by Will Evans was previously published in *Flypaper Magazine* in May 2018 and in his collection, *Still Can't Do My Daughter's Hair* (Button Poetry, 2017).

Contributors

Columbus native **STEVE ABBOTT** was a founding member in 1984 of The Poetry Forum, now the city's and state's longest-running poetry series. His poems are informed by nearly 50 years of activity in the city's political and cultural life as well as by jobs that have included landscaper, alternative newspaper editor, delivery truck driver, courtroom bailiff, private investigator, social service PR director, and college professor. His poems have appeared in dozens of literary journals and multiple anthologies, and he edited the anthologies *Cap City Poets* (Pudding House, 2008) and *Everything Stops and Listens* (Ohio Poetry Association, 2013). He has published four chapbooks, a live CD, and two full-length collections, *A Language the Image Speaks: Poems in Response to Visual Art* (11thour Press, 2019) and *A Green Line Between Green Fields* (Kattywompus Press, 2018). In 2016 he served on the Ohio Arts Council panel selecting Ohio's first poet laureate.

HANIF ABDURRAQIB is a poet, essayist, and cultural critic from Columbus, Ohio. His poetry has been published in *Muzzle, Vinyl, PEN American,* and various other journals. His essays and music criticism have been published in *The FADER, Pitchfork, The New Yorker,* and the *New York Times.* His first full-length poetry collection, *The Crown Ain't Worth Much,* was released in June 2016 from

Button Poetry. It was named a finalist for the Eric Hoffer Book Prize and was nominated for a Hurston-Wright Legacy Award. With Big Lucks, he released a limited edition chapbook, *Vintage Sadness,* in summer 2017. (You cannot get it anymore and he is very sorry.) His first collection of essays, *They Can't Kill Us Until They Kill Us,* was released in winter 2017 by Two Dollar Radio and was named a book of the year by Buzzfeed, *Esquire,* NPR, *Oprah Magazine, Paste,* CBC, *The Los Angeles Review, Pitchfork,* and the *Chicago Tribune,* among others. He is a Callaloo Creative Writing Fellow, an interviewer at *Union Station Magazine,* and a poetry editor at *Muzzle Magazine.* He is a member of the poetry collective Echo Hotel with poet/essayist Eve Ewing.

His book, *Go Ahead in the Rain,* a biography of A Tribe Called Quest was released in 2019 by University of Texas Press. The book became a *New York Times* bestseller. His second collection of poems, *A Fortune For Your Disaster,* was released by Tin House Books in September 2019. In 2020, Random House will release *They Don't Dance No' Mo.'* Yes, he would like to talk to you about your favorite bands and your favorite sneakers.

ANDREW WOODRUFF ANDERSON has a first, middle, and last name (in that order). He has been alive since he was born, has three cats (Summer Biscuit, Wolfgang, and Stella), and understands table utensils well enough to go to most restaurants without incident. He'd like to remind you of your infinite worth and inestimable value, and encourages you to treat people accordingly because it's just the right thing to do and it'll make you much happier overall.

GEOFF ANDERSON curated Columbus, Ohio's first poetry shows for biracial writers (The Other Box), translation (Lingua Franca), and immigration (New World). He's a Callaloo Fellow, and his chapbook, *Humming Dirges,* won Paper Nautilus's Debut Series (2017). See more of his work at www.andersongeoff.com.

RUTH AWAD is a Lebanese-American poet and the author of *Set to Music a Wildfire* (Southern Indiana Review Press, 2017), winner of the 2016 Michael Waters Poetry Prize. She is the recipient of a 2016 Ohio Arts Council Individual Excellence Award, and her work has appeared in *The New Republic, The Missouri Review Poem of the*

Week, Sixth Finch, CALYX, BOAAT Journal, Diode, The Adroit Journal, Vinyl Poetry, Epiphany, Nashville Review, and elsewhere. Her work also appears in the anthologies *Bettering American Poetry Volume 2* (Bettering Books, 2017), *The Hundred Years' War: Modern War Poems* (Bloodaxe Books, 2014), *New Poetry from the Midwest 2014* (New American Press, 2015), and *Poets on Growth* (Math Paper Press, 2015). She won the 2012 and 2013 Dorothy Sargent Rosenberg Poetry Prize and the 2011 Copper Nickel Poetry Contest. She has an MFA in poetry from Southern Illinois University Carbondale and she lives in Columbus, Ohio, with her two Pomeranians.

DAVID BREITHAUPT lives in Columbus, Ohio, where he works for two sports magazines, *The Buckeye Sports Bulletin* and the *Reds Report*. His essays and interviews can be found in the *LA Review of Books, Rumpus, Nervous Breakdown, Exquisite Corpse,* and others. He lives on the south side with an old dog.

Born in Montreal, Canada, and raised in Brookline, Massachusetts, **ROBERT COLBY** has lived in Columbus since 2015. He writes poetry and creative nonfiction.

HARMONY COX is a Midwestern essayist, humorist, and storyteller. Her work has appeared in *Narratively, Catapult, McSweeneys, Electric Literature,* and elsewhere. Her writing has been selected for Narratively's Top Ten of 2018, Story Club's Story of the Month, and other honors. She is based in Columbus, Ohio, and is a frequently featured performer at local open mics and literary events. She loves dogs, coffee, and writing things for you—yes, especially you.

NICHOLAS DEKKER gets people to call him "Dr. Breakfast" because he really loves breakfast and has a PhD. Nick is a food/travel writer based in Columbus, writing his award-winning blog Breakfast With Nick since 2007, where he documents his journeys in exploring breakfast, coffee, donuts, beer, the arts, family travel, and much more. Nick writes for *Columbus Alive,* the *Columbus Dispatch,* Experience Columbus, TourismOhio, *Columbus Monthly,* and many other publications; he also leads culinary tours for Columbus Food Adventures. For his grown-up job, he works on the marketing team of the Greater Columbus Arts Council.

DARREN C. DEMAREE is the author of eleven poetry collections, most recently *Emily As Sometimes the Forest Wants the Fire* (June 2019, Harpoon Books). He is the recipient of a 2018 Ohio Arts Council Individual Excellence Award, the Louis Bogan Award from Trio House Press, and the Nancy Dew Taylor Award from *Emrys Journal*. He is the Managing Editor of the *Best of the Net Anthology* and *Ovenbird Poetry*. He is currently living in Columbus, Ohio, with his wife and children.

WILLIAM EVANS is a writer and performer from Columbus, Ohio. He is a Callaloo Fellow, recipient of the Sustainable Arts Foundation Grant, and 2018 Spirit of Columbus Awardee. In addition to being the co-founder and editor-in-chief of Blacknerdproblems.com, William's manuscript, *Still Can't Do My Daughter's Hair*, was released on Button Poetry in the fall of 2017. His work can be found in *Rattle, The Offing, Winter Tangerine*, and other publications. His book, *We Inherit What the Fires Left*, is forthcoming from Simon & Schuster.

BARBARA FANT, originally from Youngstown, Ohio, is a minister, poet, and artist facilitator. She received her Bachelor of Arts degree in English Literature and Language Arts in 2010 and her Master of Theological Studies in 2012. She has been on three National Poetry slam teams from Columbus and has represented the city in four Individual National and World Poetry slam competitions. Her first poetry collection, *Paint, Inside Out,* was released in April 2010 from Penmanship Books of New York City when she was awarded the Cora Craig Award for Young Women Authors. She is a former employee of the Huckleberry House and Art for a Child's Safe America, working in shelters, prisons, correctional juvenile facilities, and elementary schools teaching art as a form of healing. She is also a member of ArtFluential of REACH communications, Is Said and the Advance Party, and has also been a regular performer on the radio show *Street Soldiers*. Commissioned by The Columbus Foundation, her poem "Today, Beginning Again," written for Columbus's bicentennial year can be found in *Revealed: Columbus, The Story of Us*. She works at The Columbus Foundation as the Nonprofit Outreach Administrator. Barbara considers poetry her ministry and currently worships and teaches at The Way Columbus church in Reynoldsburg, Ohio.

CHARLENE FIX is the author of *Flowering Bruno* (poems, XOXOX Press, 2006 & 2007 Ohioana book award finalist) with illustrations by Susan Josephson; *Charlene Fix: Greatest Hits* (Kattywompus Press, 2011); *Harpo Marx as Trickster* (McFarland, 2013, a study of Harpo in the thirteen Marx Brothers' films); and *Frankenstein's Flowers* (poems, CW Books, 2014). Charlene has published poems in literary magazines like *Poetry, Literary Imagination, Hotel Amerika, The Cincinnati Review, the Journal,* and *Forklift Ohio,* among others. She co-coordinates Hospital Poets, part of OSU's Medicine and the Arts initiative, is a member of the workshop and performance group House of Toast Poets, with them curating a reading series at Gramercy Books, and is an occasional activist for Middle East peace. She is an Emeritus Professor of English at Columbus College of Art and Design.

ADAM J. GELLINGS is a Pushcart Prize–nominated poet and instructor from the Northland neighborhood of Columbus. His poems have appeared in numerous journals and magazines, including *Atlanta Review, Prelude* and *Salamander,* and in the anthologies *Best New Poets 2017* and *A Rustling and Waking Within: Poems Inspired by the Arts in Ohio* (OPA Press). When he is not writing, you can find him going for walks at Sharon Woods Metro Park, getting groceries at Saraga International Grocery on Morse Road, or picking up carry-out from Lucky House in Westerville. The poem "American Folklore" was originally published online in *Prelude* magazine.

JEREMY GLAZIER is a poet, essayist, and two-time recipient of the Ohio Arts Council's Individual Excellence Award in Criticism. He has written for *Chicago Review* and the *Los Angeles Review of Books,* where you can read his essays on contemporary poetry and translations. His own poems have appeared in *Kenyon Review, Antioch Review, Beloit Poetry Journal,* and many other journals. He is Associate Professor of English at Ohio Dominican University.

STACY JANE GROVER is a lifelong Ohio resident who grew up southeast of Columbus in the countryside near the village of Carroll. She is a transgender writer and activist whose work focuses on how gender mediates spaces. Her work has appeared in *Entropy Magazine, Maudlin House, The Grief Diaries,* and *HEArt Journal.* She holds an MA in Women, Gender, and Sexuality Studies at the University of Cincinnati. You can find her chasing stray cats and drinking coffee somewhere in the Rust Belt with her partner, or at stacyjanegrover.com.

FAYCE HAMMOND (they/them) is a fat, queer, Chickasaw poet currently living in Colorado with their partner and cats, Furryosa and Martini Steve. Fayce has a master's degree from The Ohio State University in Women's, Gender, and Sexuality Studies. They are a co-founder of Columbus's Queer Community Mic and value building community. They also founded an online poetry journal, *Ink&Nebula*, which aims to build dialogue between established and emerging voices. You can find their work in the *Mantle, ellipsis...*, *Crab Fat Magazine, Muzzle Magazine,* and most recently, *Drunk in a Midnight Choir.*

JOE HESS was born and raised in Columbus and received his MA in Poetry from Miami University and his MFA from Ashland University. You can find his work in *Marathon Literary Review, The Ekphrastic Review, Lime Hawk Literary Arts Collective,* and in both 2017 released anthologies: Shabda Press's *Nuclear Impact: Broken Atoms in Our Hands* and Ohio Poetry Association's Ekphrastic collection *A Rustling and Waking Within.* His personal website has access to more of his publications at: jmhess.ink.

BELA KOE-KROMPECHER was born in Columbus but moved around a lot as child (ten schools over three states), and after following his first love to Columbus for college he quickly found his sense of self among the record shops and bars of High Street. After giving up alcohol in the early 2000s he went back to college and became a social worker partly due to his experiences and a hope of making a difference in other people's lives. He has been active in the arts community in Columbus for over 25 years as both an independent record label owner and concert promoter. His book, *Love, Death & Photosynthesis,* is forthcoming from Don Giovanni.

ROBERT LOSS is an assistant professor in the Department of Writing, Literature, and Philosophy at Columbus College of Art and Design. He is the author of *Nothing Has Been Done Before: Seeking the New in 21st-Century American Popular Music* (Bloomsbury Academic,

2017). His writing about the intersections of culture, politics, and aesthetics in American popular music has appeared in such places as the *Los Angeles Review of Books* and *PopMatters*. Since moving to Columbus, he has played in The Wells and his current band, Blind Engineer. Learn more at www.nothinghasbeendonebefore.com.

SHELLEY MANN HITE is a writer and editor living in Columbus, Ohio, with her husband and two daughters. She writes about food, motherhood, sobriety, and the Midwest. She cohosts Zero Proof Book Club, a sobriety podcast, and her writing has appeared in *Huffington Post* and *Mothers Always Write*. Find more of her writing at shelleymannhite.com.

Collecting Junior Ranger badges from National Park Service sites as a youth developed **SARAH MARSOM**'s appreciation for the past and a sense of place. Marsom works to improve the preservation movement's accessibility by empowering the next generation of community advocates and increasing the representation of lesser-known histories. If historic preservation is inaccessible, it is neither relevant nor revolutionary.

Her efforts to highlight hidden histories led to the development of the Tiny Activist Project. The Tiny Activist Project spreads awareness for influential women of the past, through hand-sewn dolls and workshops that fuse art and history. Crafting connections to the past fuels Sarah Marsom's passion for preservation and her work as a heritage resource consultant. She is a contributor to the third edition of *Historic Preservation: An Introduction to Its History, Principles, and Practice* and is a part of the National Trust for Historic Preservation's inaugural 40 Under 40: People Saving Places list.

ANNIE McGREEVY was born and raised at The Jersey Shore. She holds a BA in Literature from American University and an MFA in Creative Writing from The Ohio State University. She is the author of the novella *Ciao, Suerte,* and her short fiction has appeared in *The Portland Review* and elsewhere. She is currently a Senior Lecturer at Ohio State and is working on a novel. The essay "Five Reasons Why Every Writer Should Move to Columbus" was originally published on LitHub.

AMANDA PAGE is an essayist and educator in Columbus, Ohio.

GREG PHILLIPS is a web designer at Columbus State Community and has lived in Columbus since graduating from the Columbus College of Art and Design in 1989. Greg is involved in community organizations like the Franklinton Urban Empowerment Lab (FUEL) and the Lower Lights Church youth mentoring program. Greg enjoys cars, music, and long bike rides.

ETHAN RIVERA is the Curator of Writing Wrongs Poetry Open Mic held at Mikey's Late Night Slice in Downtown Columbus. He has been on six National Poetry Slam Teams. He was a National Poetry Slam Finalist with the 2011 Writing Wrongs Poetry Slam Team. He has also represented Columbus at the Individual World Poetry Slam in 2009 and 2012. He has two poems published at *Radius*, two recordings published with *Us 4 President*, and an article published in Black Nerd Problems. Rivera coached The Ohio State University National Poetry Slam Team in 2010, 2011, and again in 2017, and has also coached the Mosaic High School Poetry Slam team, which won the 2014 Columbus City Schools District Poetry Slam.

AMY TURN SHARP is an advertising copy director by day and a wild Bukowski poet by night. She runs a popular open mic night in Columbus, Ohio, where lots and lots of people tell her stories and secrets, and she has a chapbook you should buy. Since she was a child she has always taken people in her arms and helped them when they were sad. She is a visual artist who creates public art and murals and has headlined and participated in numerous art shows. Turn Sharp co-owns Secret Studio, an arts space in Franklinton.

MANDY SHUNNARAH is an Alabama-born writer who now calls Columbus, Ohio, home. Her essays, poetry, and short stories have been published in *Electric Literature, The Rumpus, Entropy Magazine, Mizna, The Normal School, The Citron Review, Heavy Feather Review,* and others. Read more at mandyshunnarah.com.

DAN SKINNER is an academic, activist, and hockey fan. He lives in Columbus.

MAGGIE SMITH's most recent books are *Good Bones* (Tupelo Press, 2017) and *The Well Speaks of Its Own Poison* (Tupelo Press, 2015), winner of the Dorset Prize. Her poems have appeared in the *New York Times, Ploughshares, AGNI, The Paris Review, The Best American Poetry 2017*, and elsewhere. In 2016, her poem "Good Bones" went viral internationally and was called the "Official Poem of 2016" by Public Radio International. Smith is the recipient of fellowships from the National Endowment for the Arts, the Ohio Arts Council, and the Sustainable Arts Foundation.

ROSE M. SMITH's work has appeared in *The Examined Life, Mom Egg Review, pluck!, Naugatuck River Review, Minola Review, Main Street Rag, Snapdragon, A Narrow Fellow*, and other journals and anthologies. She is author of the full-length collection *Unearthing Ida* (Glass Lyre Press, 2019) and four chapbooks, most recently *Holes in My Teeth* (Kattywompus Press, 2016). Rose is an editor with *Pudding Magazine* and completed a fellowship with Cave Canem Foundation in 2015.

HANNAH STEPHENSON is a poet and editor living in Columbus, Ohio (where she also runs the literary event series *Paging Columbus*). She is the author of *Cadence* (winner of the 2016 Ohio Chapbook Prize from the Wick Poetry Center), *In the Kettle, the Shriek*, and series Co-Editor of *New Poetry from the Midwest*. Her writing has appeared in *The Atlantic, The Huffington Post, 32 Poems, Vela, The Journal*, and *Poetry Daily*. You can visit her online at *The Storialist* at www.thestorialist.com.

JEFF SVOBODA views the expanding sports culture in Columbus as one way to measure the city's impressive growth in the 21st century. Originally from Lorain, Ohio, he attended Ohio State and worked at Columbus Sports Publications upon graduation before taking a job with the *Toledo Blade*.

FARIHA TAYYAB is an artist and global nomad currently residing in Columbus, Ohio, by way of Houston, Texas. As writer, educator, and photographer, she is known for her badassery as a social justice activist. In this way, Fariha remains committed to resistance by storytelling through her writing and photography.

With a degree in Arts in Creative Writing from the University of Houston, Fariha has received awards for her written work and continues to perform poetry, including winning first place at a university poetry slam. This year, she is working on a compilation of resistance poems and has been published in *Brown Girl Magazine, The Tempest,* and other publications.

PSYCHE NORTH TOROK is a graduate of Ohio State University. She is a writer and lover of words, language, and Nature. Her poems have appeared in *Mountain Astrologer, Common Ground,* and various anthologies including *Forgotten Women.* She lives and works in Columbus.

JEN TOWN's poetry has appeared or is forthcoming in *Mid-American Review, Cimarron Review, Epoch, Third Coast, Iron Horse Literary Review, Lake Effect, The Literary Review, Crab Orchard Review,* and others. She earned her MFA in Poetry from The Ohio State University in 2008. "In the Silent City She's Yearned" was published in her first book, *The Light of What Comes After,* which won the 2017 May Sarton Poetry Prize. "Diorama Turned to Ashes" was published in *Sweet: A Literary Confection.*

NOAH VAN SCIVER is an Ignatz award-winning cartoonist and illustrator.

MERYL WILLIAMS is an Ohio writer who loves roller derby and Rilo Kiley. She writes essays as well as cultural criticism about TV and feminism.

Born and raised in Columbus, Ohio, **TIFFANY WILLIAMS** received her Bachelors of Arts in Journalism from Otterbein College in 2005. She holds a Master's in Human Resources Management from Keller Graduate School of Management. Williams has worked as a freelance editor and writer, operations and customer service manager, and most recently in social services. After giving birth to twin boys in February 2016, she entered the work from home field. After re-committing herself to her passion—craft of writing—she most recently launched a blog titled, The Modern Blended Life (http://modernblendedlife.com/). This blog is for the mother who challenges the narrative that mothers have to be "all-mother, all the time." It is fueled by the concept of blending parts of yourself together and achieving balanced motherhood. This is showcased through her personal journey as a single mother to then a wife and stepmother to five children, including two bonus children and twin boys.

SCOTT WOODS is the author or editor of two poetry collections (*Urban Contemporary History Month*, 2016, and *We Over Here Now*, 2013) and a collection of essays (*Prince and Little Weird Black Boy Gods*, 2017), and is the award-winning organizer of Holler: 31 Days of Columbus Black Art (2017). He has been featured multiple times in national press, including multiple appearances on National Public Radio. He was the president of Poetry Slam, Inc., is the co-founder of the Writers' Block Poetry Night and has founded and curated numerous other events, including shows at Streetlight Guild, which Woods established in 2017. In April of 2006 he became the first poet to ever complete a 24-hour solo poetry reading, a feat he bested seven more times without repeating a single poem. He writes the column, "The Other Columbus," for *Columbus Alive*.

BELT PUBLISHING is a small, independent press founded in Cleveland in 2013 as a platform for new and influential voices from the Rust Belt and Midwest. We are committed to carefully edited, complex writing and believe in the power of community over analytics. Our titles have been praised by the *New York Times*, *Vanity Fair*, *Fresh Air*, *CityLab*, and numerous other publications. Our growing catalog of original titles includes four core imprints, including the City Anthology Series, which compiles essays, poems, and visual art from homegrown and expat writers about the cities they love. *The Columbus Anthology* is the fourteenth entry in the series. It takes its place on the shelf with more than a dozen other books chronicling contemporary life in the region. With this series we at Belt aim to create a documentary record by, for, and about the places we live and the people with whom we share them.

Also in the series:

The Cleveland Anthology
Edited by Richey Piiparinen and Anne Trubek

The Cincinnati Anthology
Edited by Zan McQuade

A Detroit Anthology
Edited by Anna Clark

The Pittsburgh Anthology
Edited by Eric Boyd

Car Bombs to Cookie Tables: The Youngstown Anthology
Edited by Jacqueline Marino and Will Miller

Happy Anyway: A Flint Anthology
Edited by Scott Atkinson

Right Here, Right Now: The Buffalo Anthology
Edited by Jody K. Biehl

The Akron Anthology
Edited by Jason Segedy

Rust Belt Chicago: An Anthology
Edited by Martha Bayne